GET UP AND GO

A

George H Sears

GET UP AND GO

The Autobiography of a Medical Missionary

GEORGE H. PEARSON

Get up and go . . . to Damascus
Luke 22.10
Acts

LONDON
EPWORTH PRESS

First published in 1968 by
EPWORTH PRESS
Book Steward: Frank H. Cumbers
SBN 7162 0064 3

Contents

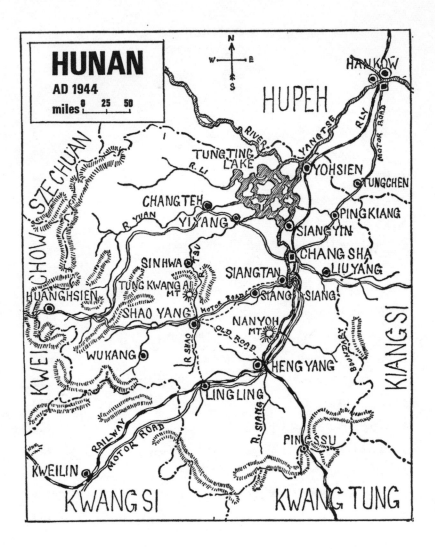

List of Illustrations

Foreword

BY THE REV. DAVID FRANCIS

MOST PEOPLE would say that this kind of book has no future. There is no longer much demand for missionary biographies, they would maintain, and for reminiscences that are now so dated. Who today wants to read about a Christian doctor's experiences in pre-revolutionary China?

I confess that I too had my doubts when I was invited to read the typescript of 'Get up and Go': doubts about the degree of interest that any such story could command today.

Yet when I started to read I was compulsively held. Why? This in itself is an interesting question. Dr Pearson would not claim to be a famous man, nor is his narrative full of hair-raising adventures and unexpected revelations. Yet many beside myself will want to go on reading to the end, once they start. Why?

I don't think there is one simple answer; there are several distinct elements which contribute to the immediate interest and abiding value of this story. One is that it concerns 'ordinary' people, and the things that happen within their ordinary lives. Another is the intimate and graphic glimpses that it gives of life in Russia at the time of her revolution, and in China before and during hers.

Yet, most of all, this book will hold the reader because it introduces us to a very real and readable person. This personal encounter is all the more impressive because it is not the writer's primary purpose. Clearly he has no desire to draw attention to himself. Yet page by page we build up an ever clearer portrait of the man.

We see him as a young lover, as a husband and a father in a relationship that was richly rewarding yet often very costly—'in sickness and in health'. We see him as a soldier of Christ simply yet completely dedicated to the doing of his Master's will. We see him as doctor, administrator, as builder and diplomat, as pastor and friend. Chapter by chapter we come to know him better, till we almost get used to—and take for granted—his energy and devotion, and his resilience under every kind of discouragement and adversity.

It would be quite wrong to get used to Dr Pearson's personal qualities, for in fact they are very rare indeed. As we follow him, first in Russia, and then for a kind of thirty years' war against disease and distress in China—and even after 'retirement', on further terms of service in Ghana and Hong Kong, in Kenya and Nigeria—we know that we are watching no ordinary man.

9

It is for this reason that Dr Pearson's challenging call to each one of us at the end of the book—to 'Get up and Go' is more daunting than perhaps he realises—for the reader will cry in his heart, 'But I am no Dr Pearson'. To me, however, the whole theme of this book is an answer to that protest. The author claims nothing in this book except that he obeyed.

Very simply he believed in trying to discern what God wants one to do, and in attempting to do just that. God directs, and as he directs He empowers. It is for us to respond with the gold of our obedience. In so far as we do just this, all things are possible. We are under 'entirely new management'. The kingship is God's, and so too is the power, and the glory.

David Francis

Brompton Regis

Author's Preface

MY JUSTIFICATION for the pages which follow must be, quite simply, that very many of my friends who have heard some small parts of the story have repeatedly, asked me to put it onto paper. This I have tried to do, using unadorned English and avoiding unnecessary adjectives or superlatives.

Living through all the changes of the two great Communist Revolutions with a full job of work to do each day, did not leave much time for writing or for the accumulation of records, but I have been able to use a number of letters written on the spot. Perhaps there was also the stimulus of living once again in the atmosphere of China in 1963, when I found myself living in a tiny Oxfam house in a refugee settlement outside Hong Kong. There I met refugees who had been my own patients years ago in Hunan. To them I was just 'another refugee' who, like themselves, had been turned out from our common home, from our own beloved Hunan. Wherever I have been I have found friends, and that Goodwill begets Goodwill.

In a record of this kind I have had to mention many people who are still with us. I hope that they will feel that I have not been ungenerous. For friends in China, I have tried to ensure a suitable anonymity without altering facts.

The reason for the title of my story may be found, perhaps, in its last few lines.

Geo. H. Pearson
'Nanyoh' 5 Church St
Chasetown, Staffs
October 1967

11

CHAPTER ONE

Together

My Start in Life

I was born at Tranmere, Birkenhead, on March 16th, 1891, my father being Charles Pearson, Junior, a younger son of a Yorkshire yeoman farming family at Yarm in the North Riding. These Pearsons had been Methodists almost since John Wesley's day.

Father was then a wholesale Provision Merchant at Liverpool in a family firm founded in 1812. He was also a keen Methodist worker. My mother was Martha Frances, daughter of George Howorth of Burnley in Lancashire. George Howorth and his brother John had been working-founder-owners of the first Burnley Cotton Mills, real Lancashire folk. Mother died suddenly from a stroke when I was still at school. Great was our loss. Ours was always a happy home.

School Days

Lessons for me began at home in New Brighton, where for a short time we had a governess for myself and my two brothers. Before long I was sent to a local preparatory school, Elleray Park, Wallasey. This was a small Anglican private school and I soon found myself the butt of much ribaldry because I was a Nonconformist and was exempted from learning the Catechism each week, though I did learn the collects and still love them. A small boy in the same school at that time was a certain Dempsey, later a Field-Marshal in the Second World War. A year or two later I went as a boarder to Woodhouse Grove School, near Bradford in Yorkshire, an old Methodist foundation, where I spent many happy days. At the Grove positive ideals of Christian service were held before us. Distinguished preachers and returned missionaries filled the school pulpit. It was in these days, supplemented by home influences, that I began to ask myself what I was going to do when school was over? How could I best serve? Could I, too, use my life for God and for others?

At this time I do not think that I ever once thought of 'expressing my own personality' or of 'bettering myself'. I wanted an opportunity to serve. I considered the Methodist ministry as a possible road, but when I heard of the need for medical mission workers abroad, that attracted me. I consulted Father. He never said much, but he did indicate that if that was in my mind, he approved, and would do what he could during the years of preparation.

A decision registered during the big evangelistic services of Torry and Alexander had its strengthening effect on my growing thinking. At the Grove there was a traditional weekly prayer meeting run by the boys themselves. In my senior years at school I came into this and it meant much.

During my years at the Grove I was always lean and lanky. My school name was 'Jade'. I was never the athletic type and I only got into the Rugger team in my last year because of my weight of bone. I began to feel that perhaps I was letting the Christian side down and must do more, for example at the summer sports. Thereafter I began to train for the mile, taking advantage of my height of six feet two inches and the length of my stride. I prayed about it too. This was a handicap race, and as an outsider I was given a generous handicap. Careful running brought me in as winner. Next year was my last at school: could I again make it a Christian witness? Again I trained and prayed. On the day, I found that I was still considered such an outsider that I again had been given a good start of 20 yards. But I notified the judges and started from scratch, on which mark there was also the Victor Ludorum of the day, T. F. Foster. As we started off I let him get into the lead while I followed closely at my own pace and stride. Coming to the last lap, I was given strength, and a spurt brought me well ahead of Foster, much to his surprise. He then did his spurt and we breasted the tape together, in a time only one fifth of a second below the school record. So pleased was the School Sports Committee with the race that they announced that this year they would give two cups for the mile race, one for each of us. I still possess mine, fifty-eight years later.

I must have been about fourteen or fifteen when Father took me to the big Overseas Missions Rally at Liverpool Methodist Central Hall. He was then the District Financial Secretary for overseas work. After the meeting I helped him to count the collection. It contained many gold sovereigns and totalled over £100. Suddenly he turned to me, saying that as he had a business engagement to go to he wanted me to take the collection home. He loaded it into a small leather bag and sent me off alone, an hour's journey by tram, ferry and tram to New Brighton, where we then lived. Did I look after that bag! I think that that must have been my very first Missionary duty.

Another inspiration of early days was at a meeting of some sort at Seacome Wesleyan Chapel, in Wallasey, during which we sang the hymn:

'When I survey the wondrous cross . . .

14

Love so amazing, so divine,
Demands my soul, my life, my all.'

As I sang those words, they just became real to me. They expressed
my own feelings and deep-down dedication and desire to serve such
a Master.

Student Days

With Father's help and a small scholarship of £25 a year for two
years only, I was able in 1909 to enter the recently established
School of Medicine at Liverpool University, travelling daily from
New Brighton. The ferry across the Mersey was always a welcome
diversion, for it was an hour's journey each way. It did not take me
long to discover the local Student Christian Movement, and its
'S.V.' section, an inner group of students eventually hoping to offer
for work abroad. The S.C.M. summer camps, first at Baslow in
1910, and later at Swanwick, were always a feast of wonder and good
things. How many friends one made as one listened, spellbound, to
William Temple, then still young and vigorous, or to Canon Scott-
Holland, to Father Kelly of Kelham, old and wise, or to Russell
Maltby, V. S. Azariah of India, or to R. O. Hall. In our Liverpool
tent we had Azariah and my friend McLeod Chisholm, an architecture student.

June 1914, and I graduated M.B., Ch.B.(Hons) with Distinction
in Surgery. That same day I was offered the most sought-after
junior hospital 'job' in Liverpool. It was due to become vacant in
three months, but it had unexpectedly fallen vacant earlier. While I
was watching the examination results posted in the University Hall,
a porter told me that the Professor of Surgery, Mr Thelwall Thomas,
wanted to see me. I found him just leaving the room where the
examiners had been meeting (I had already, like several others, put in
an application for this job).

'Have you heard you are through?' he snapped out.

'Yes, sir.'

'Do you still want the job at the Royal?'

'Yes, sir.'

'Can you start tomorrow?'

'Yes, sir,' I said without hesitation, though I had planned a three
months' holiday to start next day! So I started in at that job as
House Surgeon under him, and held it for nine months instead of
the usual six. I was at the source of some of the most thrilling and
wonderful surgery then being done by a great master-craftsman.

15

After that I transferred to the Special Departments, particularly 'Eyes', for another six months.

August 1914 — War

I was still on the junior staff at the Liverpool Royal Infirmary, and most of my colleagues were enlisting. What was my duty? At the Swanwick S.C.M. meetings and at the great Quadrennial Conference of the World Student Christian Association, I had come to know as fellow Christians students of many nations, Germans included. Must I now learn to kill these same Christians under Army orders? I had long talks, especially with my brother Norman, but we differed as to its solution. He joined the R.A.M.C. I felt that my duty lay in standing by my offer for mission work overseas, and that I must refuse to enlist. But it was soon impossible for any man of military age to leave the country.

I thus found myself one of the first great batch of Christian Objectors to Military Service. I was lonely as a 'conchie'. I got little sympathy, even in the Methodist Church, but Father understood, and our dear minister, the Rev. Joseph Whitehead, though no pacifist himself, was a tower of strength. At this time I found deep refreshment in the Friends' Meetings at Hunter Street in Liverpool, not far from the Royal Infirmary. It was there that I learned that a small group of people, Christians from many churches, had started to meet at the Friends Institute near by. I found a group of forty or fifty people, puzzled and seeking for light, in a country overrun by war fever. They called themselves the Liverpool Branch of the Fellowship of Reconciliation . . . and the rather shy secretary of the group was a recent Arts graduate of the University, Miss Mary Chisholm, sister of a friend of mine, who had come there quite unknown to myself.

Engaged — Pacifists together

Under such circumstances we soon got talking. Together we attended a weekend retreat at Hayes Farm, Clitheroe, led by Richard Roberts, a young minister later of the United Church of Canada. It seemed that Mary felt as I did about the war. She was also a lone 'objector' in her family. Her father had recently died and she was living with her mother in Birkenhead. We had some memorable walks together in the Wirral countryside, but I did not dare to say anything as yet. Eventually, I got it put down in writing and posted my proposal to her. Would she be prepared to join me in the work for which I had already offered? Would she let me try to learn to

16

love her? Her written reply reached me on a Monday morning (after a very long Sunday). It was her first 'Yes'. (Her very last words were 'Yes, yes, yes', but of that more later.) Having read this letter it did not take me long to cycle over to Birkenhead. We went for a rather shorter walk that evening in the Oxton fields and amid the cows and the sparrows we plighted our troth. She was then still wearing mourning for her father, but her black hat had a very becoming light-blue ribbon round it. From now on we would find our way in the world together—and what a world it was in 1915!

Conscription

So it was that we became two of the execrated 'C.O.s'. Together we took our decision. We could not then see what it might lead to. It is difficult now to recapture the tension of those days during the debate and passing by Parliament of those first conscription laws. Advertising to get men to join the Forces was already at its most intense and most subtle. Majority opinion was everywhere behind the Government and its war policy. People felt either the regretful necessity of a righteous war of self-defence, or that this was an opportunity for brave and adventurous action. Many Christians were just swept off their feet, puzzled and unsure. Even in the churches the line was mostly 'Stand together and resist the enemy'.

I attended one service in the Liverpool Central Hall when the Rev. Alan Holt preached a hectic recruiting sermon, which made me want to stand up in my place and contradict him in the name of my Lord. I just managed to keep quiet, but the result was to make me surer than ever of the necessity for me to follow the gleam of light that I had seen in the quiet Quaker meetings. I still loved Methodism, however, if only for its singing.

In these days of waiting for conscription to become law, none of us knew what the penalties of non-compliance might be. Loss of civil rights? Indefinite imprisonment? Compulsory enlistment and prison? These and other possibilities were all being canvassed. At last it did become law, but the work of Mr Edmund Harvey, the Quaker M.P., and others, had seen to it that a Christian objection could be recognised. Tribunals were set up to sift objectors and to deal with recalcitrants. Non-combatant units were set up under Army control and it was expected that most objectors would then go into them. But many felt that they could not accept any work for Army purposes or under Army control. Soon several Socialist 'Absolutist' objectors were being turned down and sent to the front by the Army, and even tied to the wheels of guns in action in France!

17

There were cases of ill-treatment of objectors sent for military training even as near as our own Birkenhead Park. John Leech of Liverpool, an 'Absolutist', was in prison for four years, much of it in solitary confinement.

I had earlier declined a commission in the R.A.M.C., for that was only a necessary part of the Army. I now had the opportunity of refusing my calling-up papers. I had to appear before the Wallasey Local Tribunal, who were mostly local councillors and the like. They heard me briefly and ordered 'Non-combatant service'. This I could not accept, since I would be under Army orders. I lodged my appeal. By that time I had moved on and was House Surgeon at the Victoria Hospital, Wallasey.

My appeal was fixed for an early date at Birkenhead Town Hall. I asked both my father and my minister, the Rev. Joseph Whitehead, to testify if necessary to my genuineness. This they both bravely consented to do. The Chairman of the Appeal Tribunal was a Councillor Dawson, who was also on my hospital Board of Governors. When my case was called, I was asked to state my objection to the decision of the lower tribunal. As I stood up I realized the Gospel promise that 'words will be given you to speak in time of need', for words were given to me, and I was able to speak clearly and with conviction. I had named my supporters in court, and was saying how I had already tried to get to my work in China or alternatively to work with the Friends Relief Units, but that I had been blocked by regulations, when the Chairman stopped me.

'Are you still willing to do this relief work abroad?' he asked.

'Yes,' I replied.

As I paused he consulted his colleagues and then turned to give their decision. It was 'Exempt from military service on condition that he leaves the country for work abroad within three months'. Surely a unique conditional clause!

Now we could look ahead. At first the Friends thought that they might use me in France, but their War Victims Relief Committee needed a doctor for their new refugee work in Russia, and so I was appointed to this first Russian Unit.

Over to Mary

But I find I am talking of Mary without introducing her. I wish that she herself could have written all this. She did actually make a start some years ago, but she never got beyond the first few pages.

Catherine Mary Chisholm belonged to the Clan Chisholm, originally centred round Erchless Castle, Strathglass, near Inverness.

18

She herself never lived in Scotland, but she always had a romantic affection for her clan homeland and its Scots accent.

Her grandfather, Alexander Chisholm, was one of the very first missionaries sent by the London Missionary Society to the South Seas. The story goes that he was appointed to the work while still a bachelor, but he was told he must find a wife before he sailed and take her with him! He had no one in view. He was recommended to a certain Rev. Mr Davies of Oswestry, whose eldest daughter might be willing. He went to Oswestry, but he ended by marrying the youngest daughter and carrying her off with him to the other end of the world, a long journey in those days. Many years later they returned, with a considerable and happy family. An earlier ancestor is claimed; none less than Anne Askew, the Protestant martyr under Henry VIII.

Alexander's son, John Whitridge Chisholm, married Alice Houghton of Cheshire farming stock. Their youngest daughter, Catherine Mary, was born—the youngest of ten—at Birkenhead on 6th October, 1892.

Mary was about five feet two and a half inches tall. She had a round face, friendly grey eyes and a prominent, high, but rounded, forehead, which I later learned to call the Chisholm forehead. Her hair was straight and black, or had once been black, though there were already many white strands in it before we were married, and it was quite white long before this story ends.

I had first met Mary at her home in Euston Grove, Birkenhead, when her brother, McLeod Chisholm, asked me to a family concert which they did yearly for a children's home in Dublin. She was in all the fun. Her school was Higher Tranmere High School for Girls —later destroyed by bombing. I saw no more of her until later, when I became a medical student in Liverpool and became aware that two Chisholm sisters were doing Arts in the adjacent faculty. Mary did her B.A. in education. We saw little and knew less of each other in those days. Mary held a good scholarship and she finished her course two years before I did. I was doing my House Surgeon's job when we met again, as described already.

It was after only a few months' engagement that I departed for Russia. Mary would continue living at home with her mother and go on teaching at St. Andrew's School, giving her witness on the home front.

Here are a few lines which Mary wrote to me in August 1916, not so long after my arrival in Russia. She may speak for herself:

To George

You on the Russian plain and I by the Western sea,
Does it seem a long, long way from where you are to me?
It sometimes seems to me years since we said good bye that day,
And the place where you are living seems continents away.
But at other times, my dearest, you seem quite close to me
    here,
I can almost hear you speaking and expect to find you near;
And then I seem to realize that time is nothing, nor space,
And that spirit can meet with spirit as friends meet face to
    face,
That God, our Loving Father, is as near to you as me,
So we must be close to each other, though we neither touch
    nor see,
And you in your part of His Garden and I in my corner at home,
May be used to His honour and glory that the Kingdom of
    Heaven may come.

Mary

Through Deep Water

I was away in Russia for two full years, 1916-18. We corresponded
regularly and I sent home to her, one by one in my letters, many
small water-colour sketches of the Russian scene. The album con-
taining them was a joy for years after, until it got lost and burned
during the Jap invasion of China. Only during my last few months,
when I was moving around in Russia, did I fail to get her letters.
They could not have been delivered to me anyway.

What a surprise then, on my arrival home in England, to find Mary
very worried and emotionally ill. She had not written at all during
those last three months after she had got involved with an older
member of the F.O.R. She was so confused that she could not
write to me. Things had come to a crisis just before I got home
from Russia. She had won through, helped not a little by her dear
mother, by her eldest brother Whit and by other good friends.
Amongst these, not the least was Mary Simmonds of the Methodist
Women's Settlement in Bermondsey. Mary had stopped her teaching
and seemed quite broken.

Once together again, however, we could talk and pray about it
all and God gave of his healing to us both. Years afterwards, during
our second furlough from China, Mary and I together met the man
concerned and tried to talk things out—I fear without much success.
The scars of this experience were to remain with us for life. I am

sure that Mary's later nervous breakdowns or depressions had their roots in those early days. Or had she some built-in liability to such illness?

Money was another thing which always worried her. During childhood and schooldays the family often found money in short supply. As the youngest of a family of ten she saw it all from the very close sidelines. The children rarely, or never, got any pocket-money, and her elder sisters were always advocating frugality to keep the wolf from the door. In later life she seemed to dislike handling any money, apart from day-to-day cash for the shopping. She was afraid of it.

Having grown up in a loyal Presbyterian family, Mary had also found some of the wonder at those early Student Christian Movement conferences at Swanwick. Methodism was no strange ground to her.

Our Wedding

To continue for a moment our story after my return from Russia in 1918 . . . I duly made my report of events to the Society of Friends Relief committee. They wanted me to return to Russia with a new unit, then being planned, but political and military events blocked every possibility of a passport. Our future continued very uncertain.

We therefore fixed 7th September, 1918, as our wedding day. The Rev. Joseph Whitehead came over to St Andrew's Presbyterian Church, Birkenhead, Mary's home church, for the ceremony. The guests were entertained at the home of Mary's sister, Mrs May McLean, at St Aidan's Terrace, Birkenhead.

After the wedding we left for one week of honeymoon round Bettws-y-Coed where we had good hill walks and even haymaking at Capel Curig. For our second week we moved to Bermondsey in London, where Mary Simmonds found us a room in a slum house close to the Settlement. There we had time to think and look at other aspects of life.

I now found it necessary to look for a temporary job. I discovered that looking for work does not make life easy. Whenever I have been out of work, even in my limited way, I have always found it a strain. The uncertainty and changes involved have been quite exhausting. I came to appreciate the joy of having a regular, fixed and useful job, and perhaps also to understand a little the feelings of the unemployed man in industry. This time my problem was solved by an invitation from Doctor Fox, my erstwhile chief in Russia, to join him on the staff of Lichfield Epileptic colony in Surrey.

Finally, when any permit for a return to Russia seemed to get more remote, I again contacted the Methodist Mission in London about going to China, this time two of us together. For a while we did not know whether it was to be Russia or China. We were able to have a term together at the Kingsmead Missionary Training College. Christine was born on August 30th, 1919, and shortly after that our China passport came through. Russia was still blocked—so we prepared to go as a team of three to China.

But I must go back and tell something of my days in Russia.

CHAPTER TWO

To Liubimofka

1916

The war was still in progress. Russia was already deeply invaded by German forces. Millions of people from Poland and from White Russia had fled as the fighting destroyed their homes. The various Red Cross Societies were overwhelmed with work for the wounded and could not help mere refugees. There was as yet no such thing as 'Christian Aid' for refugees.

Those who, like myself, felt unable to use the weapon of war, sought some opportunity to be not simply 'do-nothing pacifists' but rather 'Christian activists', showing our faith by what we did. It was up to us, if possible, to give not less than those who gave so much in joining the Forces.

In this situation the Society of Friends took the lead, organising first the 'Friends' Ambulance Unit' at the Front, and then the 'Friends' War Victims Relief Committee' (F.W.V.R.C.), more especially to give aid to innocent civilians, victims of the war. This was pioneer work, opening up an entirely new avenue for service. (Its effectiveness was recognized many years later when in 1947 the Friends Service Committees were awarded the Nobel Peace Prize.) This civilian relief was begun in France and in Jugoslavia. A little later two exploratory parties of senior Friends were sent to Russia to find out the position of refugees there. Their report showed great need, and to try to meet this need the first Russian Unit of the F.W.V.R.C. was equipped and sent out. I was appointed as a junior surgeon in this unit.*

On the advice of the then Imperial Russian Red Cross, we were sent to the far South-east border of Russia, because that was where the greatest number of refugees had been dumped. The refugees were mostly women and children, with a few old men. They had been boarded out on individual peasant families. Little, if any, money or food was provided for them and they were thus thrust on to the casual charity of their poverty-stricken hosts. The need was obvious.

The Unit Sails

We set sail for Norway on 14th July, 1916, divided into two parties because of submarine risks. We all wore Friends' uniform, for in

---

*Apart from my memory, what follows in this chapter owes much to the letters which I wrote to Mary while I was in Russia. There are over 100 of them, which she carefully kept. Sections in the present tense are direct quotations.

wartime no one could go anywhere or do anything without a uniform. Unit members were to get food, lodging and travel, but no other allowances. Nurses were, however, offered standard nursing pay, the wartime scarcity of nurses accounting for this.

We landed at Bergen. Thence a wonderful rail journey took us across Scandinavia and right round the north of the Baltic Sea to the border town of Harparanda. There we reached Finnish territory, where we were met by representatives of the Russian Red Cross. A few days in Petrograd and Moscow allowed us time to be shown around the royal palaces of the Kremlin.

Unit Personnel

Our numbers were not large, in all perhaps fifteen to twenty people, led by a few senior Friends. In charge of the medical affairs were Doctor and Mrs J. Tyler Fox, the latter a senior trained nurse. Miss Florence Barrow of Birmingham led the Relief work. The enthusiasm and balance of these Friends gave a tone to all the work. The rest of us were all considerably younger: in fact it has been called a Unit of Young People.

Arriving some months later, Theodore Rigg (later Sir Theodore Rigg of New Zealand) soon found his place in charge of the business affairs of the unit. He was here, there and everywhere. Local officials with whom he had to deal were amazed at his enthusiasm: 'These refugees might be his own sisters, the way he looks after them', was one Russian man's comment.

Other Unit members included one or two doctors, several young 'C.O.s' as ward orderlies, nurses and a team or relief workers, mostly women Friends. One cannot here mention all names, but one or two were outstanding. There was R. R. Ball, an English C.O. who had already worked with the unit in France, a lovely Christian character, but with no memory. He was reputed to have given his coat to a refugee, more than once, but he did not mind using other people's clothes if he could not find his own! One day he gave away his penknife and at once came to borrow mine. He died some years later in Russia, where he was still doing relief work with the Friends.

Margaret Barber was another refreshing person. Daughter of a canon of Ely Cathedral, she had already done relief work in Canada, in Serbia and in Armenia. Her description of all the canons and deans trying to get her to tell of her experiences was very amusing. She was like a schoolboy. We soon found that she could never abide 'stick-in-the-muds' or 'rich people'. Anyone who had money or possessions was to her anathema. She could be quite rude to such

24

folk, but she loved every poor person and would go out of her way to do everything possible for them. How she would repeat the Russian word for rich (bogatie) with such scorn! She had only a wartime V.A.D.'s training, but with her poor ones she was one of nature's own nurses.

When the unit eventually broke up she remained in Russia doing various nursing jobs. She married a Russian, but later lost both husband and son in the fighting and disorganization. She then settled in the Crimea, doing massage and living on a Russian Government Old-Age pension. To the end I used to get an occasional letter or picture postcard, all extolling the work of the Russian Soviet Government for the needy poor.

In August 1917 the unit was joined by a small American group of Friends, one of them of Russian extraction and speaking fluent Russian.

In my medical work I had the use of an interpreter for the first three months and had a few language lessons, but after three months I had to manage on my own.

Buzuluk

Buzuluk (the name is of Tartar origin) is a small prairie town, the centre of administration of one of the divisions of the Samara (later Kuibischeff) Province. It lies ninety miles south-east of Samara, half way along the main railway to Orenburg and Tashkent in Central Asia. The village of Liubimofka lies eighty miles (120 versts) to the south of Buzuluk, across the unpaved mud roads over the steppe. For this part of the journey we were granted the use of Government post-horses and tarantass. The tarantass is a four-wheeled cart of basket work, whose only springs are the two fir tree poles which unite the two axles.

In winter the tarantass gives way to the sledge, a similar basket, fixed to runners and horse-drawn. When well padded with straw these baskets make a not uncomfortable vehicle. I have been much less comfortable in many later motor trucks or buses.

In winter, when the temperature might register anywhere down to −40 centigrade, it could be cold on these trips. The unit provided each worker with a heavy peasant sheepskin overcoat or 'shuba' for winter wear. These, with the fleece inside, are warm, but when new smell like bad cheese. For a long drive in really cold weather, there was a second sheepskin overcoat or 'tooloop', made big to wrap round everything. This was not individual clothing but part of the unit equipment. Leather boots were far too cold and restricting for winter wear. We always used the Russian valenki, boots of thick, porous, felted sheepswool. A Russian style fur hat completed the ensemble.

Liubimofka

Liubimofka (pronounced 'Lioo-bee-moff-ka' with the accent on the 'bee') is the name of a large village where I lived and worked for eighteen months of my two years in Russia. It was the first and main centre for our medical work.

It consists of two long rows of wood or mud-built huts all facing on to a mile-long, very wide, unpaved mud street. The smaller huts often have only one small piece of glass built into the wall to let in a little light. The larger huts are of logs, with better double-glazed windows and a roof of green-painted sheet iron. Alongside each home is a large yard door opening on to a farmyard where the cattle and horses live and where all the farm work is done.

At intervals along the street is an open well, and beside each well stands a tall pole with a cross-beam balanced on it, weighted to make easy the lifting of buckets from the deep well.

Near the centre of the village the street becomes even wider, to accommodate the market place, where a number of shops are housed in wooden shacks or shanties closely huddled together. On market days the whole place is alive with peasants buying and selling wheat, millet, potatoes, cabbages or fuel. Everyone bargains for everything. Long and heated are the arguments before the inevitable bargain is struck. The shops sell a bit of everything. One or two specialize in cotton cloths and prints of every hue. You can, if lucky, buy a spade or some biscuits, a looking-glass or an envelope, a cake of soap, a paraffin lamp or some knitting wool, a fur hat or a sample tin of Allenbury's food. If one shop has not got what you want, perhaps next door may have it! Perhaps not—or they may get it 'soon'—that wonderful Russian word 'sechass' means 'this year, next year, sometime, never!' Or even 'at once!'.

The Church

Overshadowing everything else is the village church. It is a large, white-painted wooden building with magnificent silver domes on its towers, and many pinnacles and small spires. Inside there are no seats—everyone stands. The walls are covered with many realistic paintings of scriptural scenes. At services a beautiful choir always sings unaccompanied and incense fills the building.

26

I was told by a peasant that this lovely church had been built only a few years earlier after they had lost the former one by fire. It had cost them thousands of roubles, but having had a bumper harvest, everyone had helped, and it was done. They also have a fine bell.

At service times the church is crowded, men in front, women towards the back, all standing and devoutly crossing themselves. The old Slavonic language is still used, though none understand it. As I stood there in the crowd the sun was shining across the front of the congregation, its slanting beams made visible by the clouds of sweet smoke from the incense. I felt quite able to worship with these simple folk.

The people of Liubimofka are 'Great Russians'. Their agriculture is so poor that they get little return for their hard work. Some other local villages have quite different racial origins. One is Tartar, another is Ukranian and has much higher standards. Winter here is long, the snow lies for six months in the year. All the field work has to be done in the summer half of the year, but if the melting snow can be used and the rains are good it is very fertile prairie land. But famine and drought are ever-present threats. The sudden dumping on to these poor peasants of whole families of refugees, some to every household, was in itself unmitigated tragedy.

The Refugees

Women, children and a few old men fled before the dreaded German armies as they advanced into Russia. They had been crowded into trains and cattle trucks and after weeks of travel had been dumped here, there and everywhere. Often families got separated and lost. A typical story was told to me: a mother and her children were on one of these trains. The father had been taken for the war. At one station the train started as the eldest girl was on the platform. Mother jumped out to try to find her girl, but the train went on. She never found that eldest girl, but in some marvellous way she was able to catch up with the others and find them, but by then all their baggage had been stolen. Here she was in Liubimofka, still doing what she could for her little ones.

When we arrived, winter was rapidly approaching. We found it impossible to buy food or fuel in the large quantities needed for relief. Some clothing was obtained and distributed. Cash distribution was ruled out as undesirable for many reasons. Work was what these people wanted. If they could work and earn something they could find a way to get what they most needed. Various industries were tried by our relief staff. Finally, it was spinning, hand-loom weaving and traditional peasant embroidery that proved most feasible. Always a few of the refugees were 'difficult': they had lost so much they felt they had a right to this or that, and lots more of it. Most were exceedingly patient and grateful.

Our relief workers organized these workshops in quite a number of villages and made them very effective, but this was not the side of the work of which I saw most.

Peasant Life

The season of Lent brings to these people a real eight-week fast during which not even milk or eggs may be eaten by the faithful. They then live on bread, potatoes and a few available local vegetables. But when the fast is over they make up for lost time. Easter is the greatest of these great Feast Days or 'Prazdneeks'. All work stops for days together. Even suitable rains for the spring sowings are neglected, or good harvest weather. Everyone puts on his best new coloured shirt and comes out to have a good time. The long and crowded church services are soon over and there is plenty of time for singing and dancing, for buying and selling, or whatever takes the fancy.

As I read my Russian New Testament, I could see Jesus coming into this village on such a holiday, everyone busy feasting and gossiping. All would be talking of this strange man who had come to their town. 'But they say he is the Nazareth carpenter's son!' What opinions they would express and how such a crowd might be swayed. See how they all come uninvited into the small house where he is, looking at everything, joining in all the conversation, though possibly quite unknown to the owners of the house. No-one would think of turning a guest out, everyone is friendly . . . how it all comes to life.

These days that I lived in Russia were still long before the era of radio or television. People still made their own amusements and really enjoyed life.

One day a peasant walked into my room saying: 'Come along, the feast is starting. Come, and bring your music too', referring to my fiddle. We followed him and found that we were in for a real wedding feast. Here the bride often does the proposing. We heard of one young man who had had several offers. But when he takes his bride he has to pay something to her parents for her. This bridegroom told us that he had had to pay 140 roubles, a big sum in these days, for his new wife. His father then chimed in: 'I only paid 14 roubles for mine—got her cheap, but I've been able to put her right and she's as good as any wife now'—this before all the company. The feast went ahead with music from an accordion, and I had to play more dances on my violin.

The great Easter Church Services, so often described, are the culmination of the Church Year. On Maundy Thursday at 10 p.m., comes the reading of the twelve portions of scripture. As the priest reads, the people nearest to him light their candles from his and pass the light to those near, so that very soon, the 'light of the gospel' fills the whole church. Or there is the final service beginning near midnight on the Saturday, in which an empty coffin is carried round the church and everyone greets everyone else with the phrase 'Christos voskress' (Christ is risen), to which comes the reply: 'Vo eestino voskress', (He is risen indeed), and the Christian kiss is exchanged.

The Hospital

The district Hospital at Liubimofka, which we took over, is a small, isolated group of log-built houses, inside its own ring-fence, at the east end of the long village street: having been built by the old District Council as a Medical centre for all the surrounding villages, but it had been closed due to the war and lack of staff. Accommodation consisted of: Doctor's bungalow, Dispensary with two flats above, Surgical ward with theatre, Infectious diseases ward, also bakehouse, Russian bath house, a well, and a stable with cellar icehouse underneath. In the Dispensary we found a fair stock of drugs, all labelled with German names. One or two old hospital servants were still there as caretakers.

After our arrival we received an early visit from the District Council Chairman, the 'Mareschal de Noblesse', who arrived in his old car, the only car we ever saw during our two years in the district. He was very much interested in our work and particularly anxious that we should take over the medical care of local inhabitants as well as the refugees. We were thus responsible for an area the size of Cheshire, with a large and very scattered population.

Patients were soon crowding our daily clinics. For the first three months I had the help of an interpreter. Thereafter I had to carry on as well as I could in my broken Russian. Even simple question and answer had its difficulties, for there were no clocks and few calendars in the village. Time was fixed by four events of the day— Sunrise, Dinnertime (or noon), The coming home of the cows, and Sunset. To fix a day it was necessary to say so many days before, or after, the nearest church festival. For example: 'Four days before Ascension, at the time of the cows coming home, our Ivan said he

29

hurt his leg', etc.   Most of the folk here look so old.   A woman of twenty looks thirty or thirty-five, and the universal beards make the men look old.   One old man who came to see me claimed to be ninety, and had fought as a Russian soldier in the Crimean War! He had cataracts.

Wind and Snow

A constant feature of our work at Liubimofka was the requests for visits to sick folk at outlying villages.   In summer this meant long drives by tarantass or cart.   In winter it was by horse-drawn sledge, going for many miles across the apparently untrodden snow.

One night, returning from a late trip to Bagdanofka when snow lay thick and the road was unmarked by any hedges or branches, my driver was only a small boy—all men were at the war.   He just gave his horses their heads.   Thus they often find their own way back by feeling with their feet whether they are on the hard track hidden by the thick untrodden snow.   It was eerie, driving thus from nowhere to nowhere through an inky blackness.   Snow everywhere.   Occasionally there is a patch of earth, blown clean of snow.   You wonder if you are coming to a village; then it suddenly comes up to you.   You pass by and again the same blackness all around.   Finally another darker mass, and suddenly, there is a tiny, lighted window in a small outlying hut.   Then come several big bumps as the sledge slides over the trodden snowdrifts of the village street.   You are home again!

On another occasion in 1917, I had been called to visit the wife of the priest at Logachofka, twenty-five versts away.   It was March and near the time for the snows to melt.   I finished my usual Out-patients clinic early, perhaps seventy patients, had lunch and set off with an Austrian prisoner as driver.   We arrived without incident. I saw the patient and had an interesting talk with the priest, who was interested in China.   He fed us well and asked us to stay overnight as the weather was looking bad; but my driver (who had no local knowledge) and I both wanted to get home.   I had to be at Bagdan-ofka for a clinic next morning.

As we started out, the wind was still strong, and now it would be in our faces.   It soon increased, lifting the snow right onto us.   I was able to sit fairly comfortably in the sledge with my face sideways to the wind, with my big fur collar up.   It was already dusk, when I distinctly saw two large animals, perhaps a quarter mile or more away, moving on the snow and apparently taking cover here and there.   They made no attempt to come up with us.   They could only be wolves, as these exist in this district.   However, they were soon lost to sight in the blowing snow and gathering storm. It is a lonely road. Only one isolated hut to be seen in all the twenty miles. We drove on. Dusk passed into the greyness of night. We could see nothing but the road at our feet. Even the tree branches set in the snow every fifty yards or so were invisible till we could almost touch them. The blowing snow stuck to the fur of my up-turned collar to form a snow veil right across my face, with a small opening to look out of and breathe through. How my driver managed to see anything I don't know. It was a strange feeling out there. I remembered Tolstoy's story, *Master and Man*, where he tells of two men lost in the snow, only his tale was one of mid-winter when the thermometer is at its lowest.

At length we reached the top of a rise and could see one or two distant village lights, but then there were new dangers; for the unfenced track at this point skirts some deep, open sand-pits, ten to twenty feet deep, and now filled level with soft snow. Our only way was to try to see that our horses kept rigidly to the hard-worn track which we could not see!

Our eventual arrival back at the hospital was quite unexpected in such a 'bouranne', as they call these storms of blowing, soft, quick-melting snow. Next day I got off to Bagdanofka on time, but these journeys do need faith.

On another trip, when crossing a small frozen stream, my two horses suddenly fell through the ice and lay down in two and a half feet of icy water. The sledge remained miraculously high and dry. The driver waded in, released his horses from the shafts, got them upright, turned the sledge round and proceeded to find a better crossing place.

Another time, having been delayed by an urgent call, I arrived at our Bagdanofka dispensary at 2 a.m. I opened the door and just went to sleep on the dispensary floor, with the aid of the two fur coats that I was wearing and a rough straw mattress. I was discovered next morning by the two American women relief workers, who came in to prepare for their own day's work. The doctor having arrived, the place was soon crowded with patients and I was kept busy all day. On another occasion I awoke with a splitting headache, due to a charcoal stove left in the room to warm me—carbon monoxide poisoning.

Morgatova Village

During the summer of 1917 I was in charge of the dispensary at Morgatova, north of Buzuluk. This village was very different from those in the south because it was in an area of old high pine forest. The spring flowers in the forest glades are never to be forgotten, violets, lily-of-the-valley, forget-me-nots and the like. But always the main interest here was the large Children's Home set up and run by our relief workers in a big old chateau, for some of the most desperate children. And sometimes mother was also brought in, to work on the domestic staff.

Children coming here from their life of wild neglect, were not naturally clean or tidy next day. My first impression was one of the freedom and general happiness of the place. The children look up and smile. None of the old cringing and scraping. Sanitation has been a big problem, but Miss Barrow is bent on making the children both happy and clean. In their own homes, mother sews on the child's clothes each autumn and there they stay—regardless—till next summer. Here the weekly bath is compulsory. Orderlies Collis and Welch, both scout-masters, were in their element. Heads were shaved, scabies cured and new clothes all round was the order.

The Russian language is phonetic and I soon found that I could get a Russian fairy-story book and sit down and read it aloud to my small friends, even though I could not understand it all myself. During my two and a half months at Morgatova I got very much attached to these lovely children and was loath to leave when the Unit again needed my services in Liubimofka.

Here too, I had many out-calls. One day I was called to a case forty versts away through the forest. I started with one tired-out horse in the tarantass shafts. I soon had to get out and walk. We arrived at a posting station but the post-master would not provide a change of horses. Finally I did get just one horse and an almost blind old man as driver. It was already dark when we got started again. The driver could see nothing in the dark and gave his horse its head. Before long he had quite lost the track. I got out, but only by feeling for the track crawling on my hands and knees in the forest glade in the dark did I manage to find it again. It was now raining. Would we have to sleep out till morning? I now took the horse's head myself, feeling for the trodden track with my own feet and using eyes and ears for what they were worth. The old man remained on his driver's box, comforting me by saying how well he knew the road! We had to negotiate two narrow unfenced wooden bridges before arriving at our destination at one a.m. . . . to find the maternity case all happily over and my services not needed.

That night I was housed in the spare room of a wonderful old chateau, the residence of a former member of the Duma (the

32

Tsarist Parliament). His wife was still there, but farm and buildings had all been pillaged, everything was in ruins. It was a sad glimpse into what had been.

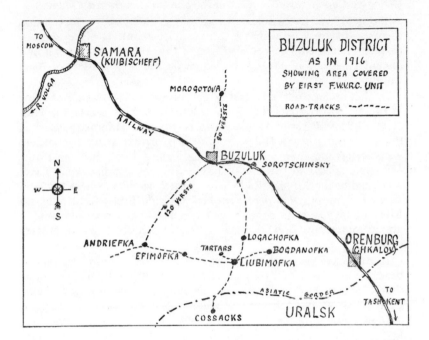

CHAPTER THREE

Revolution 1917

Changing Conditions. The Russian Revolution seen from a Village.

Although I lived in Russia all through the great Bolshevik Revolution there is strangely little that I can recount about its big events, or its prominent people. For all through those days I was living in a distant village, way beyond the Volga on the very borders of Asia, Liubimofka.

In that village, our very first direct news of what was afoot came at the end of March 1917, when Doctor Fox returned to the Unit after a business trip to Moscow and Petrograd. He was there when the first rioting began and when different revolutionary committees were struggling for power and when Prince Lvoff became Prime Minister. Fox had met Lvoff only a few days earlier when Lvoff was head of the Russian Red Cross. Hotel windows where Fox and Tatlock were staying were smashed by rifle fire. Returning via Moscow they were in contact with the Tolstoyans and were able to attend a meeting of 300 released conscientious objectors to military service!

It must have been only a few days before Fox's return that we had been told quite casually by one of our Austrian P.O.W. servants that the Tsar had 'resigned'. A printed proclamation was being posted everywhere. Life in the village went on as usual.

It was not until April 1st, 1917, that I wrote home: 'We have had a revolution in our village now. The "Headman", his assistant and the village secretary have all been dismissed, and of course, the village constable too. He was known as the "Strazhneek", the "Terrible One" or the "Frightener", a known bully of helpless peasants.

'We are now ruled by a "Provisional Committee" whose Chairman acts as "Headman". In Andriefka a similar committee has elected its lady schoolteacher as "Headman". Later the Committee was called "The Committee of the People's Power". Here in Liubimofka the schoolteacher has become the "village secretary" and is quite the brains of the village. I had tea with her and was invited to come with her to a meeting just starting, which was to be the first ever meeting in this village of the "All Russian Union of Peasants". I was given a seat in the centre beside the Chairman and, listened with interest, being able to understand some speakers better than others. It was something like an election meeting at home, but everything had to be very simple for the peasant audience. For instance they had to explain the difference between a Monarchy and a Republic, and to define what Liberty meant. The meeting duly adopted the programme of the Union, which included such things as a desire for Republican Government, liberty of worship, but not destruction of the church, a fair division of the land, the abolition of the old passport system, and a desire for peace because "war costs too much".'

September 1917. 'We now have a "Village Food Committee". The village is facing famine this winter. This committee was elected by "The Committee of the People's Power" and seems to be a selection of its worst and most ignorant peasants. The Chairman is a Tartar, who changed to Christian, then back again to Tartar, so that now no-one trusts him. The first thing that this Food Committee did was to vote themselves salaries at a high rate. The villagers objected so they withdrew the vote, and proceeded to get their salaries by less obvious means. As a result of their thus well-paid labour sugar has become unobtainable, and the stock of bread or flour in the village is now so low that each person can now have only 15 funt (5 pounds approximately) of flour this month, last month it was 40 funt, and next month they do not even know where the 15 funt is to come from. Already there is a call for a new Food Committee.

'Ideas are spreading as to the abolition of all private property. Crown land has already been distributed. There is talk of taking back any "excess" from those who have bought land with their savings and even of levelling round the excess bank balances in private accounts!

'The sad thing is that the big farmers have always obtained so much more per acre from their holdings as compared to the peasants with their old-fashioned ways. . . yet it sometimes looks as though the rich will still find ways of keeping rich still!

'As for ourselves, we have so far been able to buy enough of the necessities of life for winter use, and so can carry on, but prices are queer things these days.'

December 1917. 'Yesterday was the day of the very first elections in our village. There was not much excitement. The system is simple. There are sixteen competing parties; each has a number. All the voter has to do is write the number of his party on a paper and drop it into the ballot box. All votes from all over the province are then lumped together, and each party gets so many members chosen from the provincial party list. Our peasants all voted for Party

No. 3—the "Social Revolutionary and Peasants Deputies Combined Party".'

Later, December 1917. 'There have been strange doings in the village today. The Committee has suddenly requisitioned (without any payment) all corn, flour, cattle and agricultural implements from the larger farmers. They may retain only two cows, one horse, one plough. Nothing more. But now the Committee does not know what to do with the cattle they have got! Should they sell them for cash or kill them for meat? Or distribute alive to poorer peasants who have none? Any returned soldiers here are helping the Committee, which seems to be acting on "Social Revolutionary Party" instructions. It is done quite impersonally. It is interesting—but can it work? Meanwhile confusion is worse confounded. And starvation is near.

'We only hear rumours of what is happening in the big towns. What a lack there seems to be of any spiritual background. How is the love of Jesus so sorely needed in this situation?'

February 1918. In Buzuluk town. 'Here in town the new Bolshevik Regime continues to keep its reputation for energetic work. By a new decree everyone must clean the road daily in front of his house or be fined 100 roubles. There is now separation of Church and State. Two priests preached against this decree and were arrested, this resulted in rioting and a curfew. The word "Comrade" (Tovarich) is in use on every possible occasion.

'Railway journeys are a special hazard. Nobody now worries about tickets—soldiers especially, as no-one can control them—so everyone just pushes in his baggage and sits on it and listens to the conversation all round.

'Porters at the stations still exist, but only work for colossal tips, yet it has been proposed that porters be abolished "Because a poor man never needs a porter". Every wandering soldier takes it upon himself to be a plenipotentiary of the government. They are crude, but are often helpful to the poor. If you meet a bad one, who fancies you to be rich, you have no redress. The story goes that a group of men stopped a well-dressed man in the street and demanded his coat. "Well," was his reply, "I suppose I've got to give it to you, but I only took it from another man yesterday." "Oh," was the reply, "you are one of us, are you? Keep the coat, Comrade."

'Minds are wide open, except that they are quite sure that everyone is out to get what he can for himself. A charitable organization like ours is quite beyond their comprehension. The big shops have all been dismantled and sold out. To buy some cooking-oil for the refugees at Morgatova, Collis recently found that he needed special permits from seven different Comrades before he was allowed to buy it.'

Our last winter in Liubimofka

Famine was with us. Many of the refugees had already been moved on, but the local need for help was greater than ever. Doctor and Mrs Fox had been invalided home, so I was left in charge of the hospital with Margaret Barber as nurse, Hinman Baker as orderly and odd-job man, and Esther White (U.S.A.) as Relief Helper. Snow storms continued so that we had drifts ten feet high all round our hospital buildings and often had to dig ourselves out. At the great Annual Fair in October there had been plenty of cabbages to buy for salting down, but no flour or potatoes at all. Cattle, horses and camels were being sold for a song. There was no fodder for them. The remaining horses were already just skin and bone. We were finding it very difficult to get horses for our frequent journeys.

To quote again: 'Even village society seems to be breaking up. Robberies for food have become common. Twice our store-room has been rifled. Recently two men came to me threateningly asking me to engage them instead of the present servants! The village deacon feels that everything is going wrong and is hopeless. Any man who can do so is driving South to Cossack-land to buy food. He whose horse is too weak just cannot find bread. One old man tells me that every day he has to struggle to make his starving horse stand up, so that it will try to eat some of the old dry straw which is its only food. Another is feeding his horse on the straw from his old thatched roof.'

'The war is over. We are all cut off. It is time for us to go home.' On March 12th, 1918, 'I received an official request to attend a meeting of the Village Soviet, now the only Authority here. It is their "order" that we shall not leave the village. They need us here . . . Esther White and I answered the summons. They had sent a special sledge for our convenience. We found that the meeting was being chaired by a sailor, recently home from the Baltic Fleet and we were given seats of honour next to him. He then made his speech. Could we not stay with them longer? Why were we going? Was it because of the recent thefts?'

In reply I had to explain our position and how we had already made all arrangements with the medical authorities in Buzuluk. As we could no longer carry on they had promised to find staff to take over from us next month.

37

The meeting then resolved itself into one to find ways of thanking 'the English Mission' for work done. 'Would you', they asked, 'find it right by your beliefs if we bought you each a little Ikon as a memento?' We gave our consent and I was able then and there, while thanking them, to try to explain fully the spiritual basis which had lain behind all the service which the Unit had given in their village, quite an impromptu sermon. It was the only time in all our years in Russia that I really had such a chance of telling the Gospel story.

The clerk carefully asked for our full names, so that he could write the letters of thanks properly. A few days later a special deputation arrived from the Soviet with the letters and the Ikons, one for each of us, and expressing their wish that the Ikons might preserve us for many years of work for the poor and needy.

In 1968 I still have my Ikon as bright and shining gold as ever.

'But in so many matters disorganisation still reigns in the village. The Chairman is constantly being changed. Every day the muddle grows' . . . And at this stage we had to leave.

Russian Sectarians and Pacifists

One of the first happy effects of the Revolution was the new freedom of speech everywhere. When we arrived in Russia under the Tsar we had been warned to stick to our jobs and to refrain from criticism of either Church or State. Under the new regime everyone could say just what he thought. Also I myself, was gradually becoming more vocal in the use of the language, and we began to get occasional contacts with people with unorthodox views.

It was when I was in Andriefka, after leaving Liubimofka, that I heard of a small colony of 'Molokani' in the district. The name means 'Milk drinkers', as they are a Christian body who allow the use of milk during the great Church fasts. The Orthodox Church forbids such use. I met one of their leaders who told me that they have several families in a village thirty versts from Andriefka, where there are also a few Dukhobors, who also call themselves 'Kuakeri' or Quakers!

The Molokani are Independant Evangelical Christians. They tell us that they reject all ritual, and believe just what they read in their Bibles. All are equally Brethren; Jesus is their only priest. They believe that all war is wrong and will not fight. Some of their men were taken away by the Army, but they refused to take the military oath even under threat of shooting, for they also believe all swearing to be wrong. They teach that a man's works must correspond

38

with his faith, his faith being useless if accompanied by bad deals. Their marriage ceremony is delightfully simple. One or two prayers; a promise before the congregation to be true to each other, after which the bride's father takes her hand and gives it to the bridegroom. Then another reading and a prayer.

I was able to attend one of the Molokani meetings for worship. Present were six men, three women and two of us. We all sat round the dining table as passages of scripture were read. Any member might read and everyone kept up a flow of comments on almost every verse. Then came chanted psalms or Bible passages. The singing was weird. No one had any idea of a tune. Finally more prayers, but even here everything must be in the exact words of scripture, for they do not trust any later writers. They have no preacher and no sermon. Their Bibles are in both the old Slavonic and in Russian.

Later five of them attended our own Quaker meeting and said that they had heard some of our hymns in a Russian Baptist Service. In the past these people have been much persecuted by the authorities. Now they are free. Though genuine Christians it does seem that these Molokani are in a backwater, shut off from all other Christians by persecution and by their physical isolation in these Steppe villages.

One of them told me that twenty years earlier Tolstoy himself used sometimes to come to their big meeting. My informant had himself met him there. He arrived on horseback, wearing his rough peasant shirt of 'sackcloth', but he never went to the Orthodox Church.

Tolstoy

One day a rich peasant asked Tolstoy, 'What is your faith?' Tolstoy replied, 'My faith is to buy wheat for 50 kopeks and then sell it to a poor man at 30 kopeks'. My friend commented that probably that rich Orthodox peasant used to buy it for 50 and then sell it for 100 kopeks. They told me that Tolstoy used to come down to this area to work in the summer. His deeds were good. On one occasion Tolstoy heard that there had been persecution and that some of the Molokani children had been taken away from their parents to be 'educated'. He complained about it in St Petersburg, and sure enough when he came next year the children were all happily back in their homes.

During our time in Liubimofka I met two or three isolated men who claimed to be Conscientious Objectors, one, a strict Baptist who had lived for a time in New York, and who had been flogged in Russia for his faith. When he got to America he was much surprised to find that their Bible was the same as his Russian one. That induced him to study it as he has done. We parted with a Russian kiss, the ancient Christian greeting.

Another refugee C.O. whom I met, was one of our carters at Liubimofka, his name was Philip. He thought there were 7,000 Objectors in Russia. He had been conscripted more than once but was released to supply millet. He might be called up again, but is very steadfast and hopeful. He said that many C.O.s like himself had been reasonably treated by their officers, though their offence could mean exile to Siberia, or worse. His wife remained in Liubimofka, but possibly he was again conscripted. We had no news.

Fire

Only a few months after our arrival in Liubimofka we had a disastrous fire, losing the whole of our surgical block, fortunately no lives were lost. Its cause was a spilt paraffin lamp while Collis, our orderly, was trying to repair the frozen water supply in the roof space. He was helpless. Soon the church bells were ringing and the local hand-fire-engine and water-carts appeared, but they were powerless too. As the flames rose higher I began to fear for the next building, fifteen yards away across the snow and in the track of the flames. I started to organize a water supply to save this other ward, refusing to let the crowd have my water for the burning building and generally acting as policeman. It was market day so we had a big crowd. When the roof fell in there was a tremendous flare-up, the flames just leaping towards the second block and the heat was so great that my water supply was now almost unapproachable. Some local Tartars and Austrian prisoners, however, ran in with buckets, one even pouring water over himself first to keep cool and the second ward, though charred, was saved. At this point I could do no more and I retired for a quiet prayer. When I got back again all was fully under control.

When we reported the fire to the Medical Authority in Buzuluk, they replied 'Nichevo'—'it is nothing'. 'We often have fires in Russia.' Some of the half-burned logs came in very useful later on to augment our winter fuel supply.

Over a year later, when I was at Andriofka, we had another similar fire, due this time to careless stove lighting by our local handyman. These two fires together have left me with quite a marked subconscious fear of fire—and a healthy respect for its powers.

CHAPTER FOUR

The Long Road Home

It was already late spring in 1918. The general social disorganisation everywhere in Russia continued, but the new regime was beginning to function. Already we had succeeded in handing our small Steppe hospitals over to the newly organised Revolutionary Government. Our nurses had left for home. I was out of a job. No letters were coming through from England, and no funds.

Many of the children from the Morgotova Orphanage had already been removed by relatives who were trying to make tracks for homes in White Russia or Poland. A newly established Government Orphanage in an old monastery at Buzuluk was willing to take care of those who literally had no home. Buzuluk itself was crowded with refugees all trying to get on the first train for the West. But no trains were running, or almost none. The people were rapidly coming to the end of their meagre food supplies and funds. The large railway stations were all crowded with camping passengers, waiting, just waiting. We had no money or food to distribute to such crowds, but wondered whether possibly some sort of relief workshop in the town could be got going, but what the refugees now wanted was transport—not work.

Fourth Class to Saratoff

The Unit had received a bank draft from London for £1,000, but no bank in either Buzuluk or Samara had enough cash available to honour it! But they told us that if we could take the draft to Saratoff, further South, the bank there had cash and might be able to help us. I was therefore, asked to go alone with the draft on the long journey to Saratoff, travelling on the always crowded refugee trains and by boats on the Volga. Samara station was filled by 3,000 or 4,000 refugees, and when any train was sighted it was a case of push and get on if you can! While in Samara I witnessed one of the early great 'International May Day' demonstrations. It was a compulsory holiday for everyone. Banners and slogans of every sort were carried in a huge procession. Even the Anarchists were prominent with their 'all-black' flags. But they were suppressed very soon after by the Bolsheviki. Free German and Austrian soldiers (P.O.W.s) carried banners 'We love the International' and sang the Marseillaise as they passed. What a scene! Will these men ever get home?

From Samara my route was south on the Volga River. I was able to book a second-class ticket on the boat but could only get a stiff chair on which to pass the night. I looked around and found plenty of floor space in the fourth class steerage. I therefore put on my big sheepskin coat and my blanket and had a fine night's rest. I only woke in the morning to find the seamen washing the deck and I almost rolled over into the swill.

Arrived in Saratoff, a provincial capital, I somehow found lodgings in a room in a back street. It took me the next seven days of hard work to get that draft cashed. The banks were helpful, but needed high-up authorisation. All offices only opened at 11 a.m. and closed at 4 p.m. Many were the officials whom I needed to contact. One introduction to a lady at the head of the Commissariat for Social Service proved very helpful, but many other signatures were still needed. Not until seven days later, just as 4 p.m. struck, was I able to accept cash from the bank, all in new Communist 100 rouble notes. Back in my digs I hastily used needle and thread to sew the bulky stuff into the outside pockets of my Friend's Uniform, trusting to its very bulk to make it unlikely that anyone would spot what I was carrying. Then down to the riverside and on to the next boat travelling upstream—again fourth class. I was indeed much relieved when I could hand over my burden to Rigg in Buzuluk —the very last remittance from London that our Unit was able to handle.

The Unit then gave me orders for home. Four of us were to go to Moscow by river. Alas, I had this time to leave my beloved old sheepskin coat behind, as Gregory Welch had used it when he got mild smallpox. Hearing of the famine in Moscow, we each bought as much bread as we could carry at villages en route. This proved a great boon later on.

Moscow

In Moscow every hotel was crowded to the doors. Eventually, Count Sergei Tolstoy and his wife found us a room in their home at Bolshoy Levshinsky Perioolok, 15. Countess Olga Tolstoy introduced us. We would be paying guests, for the present prices of food made anything else impossible. 'Only 2¼ ounces of the very coarsest black bread could be had daily on the ration. Rich and poor alike are glad to get even that. For any other food one must hunt in the peasant markets and pay fantastic prices. Life is hard these days.

'The house itself is an old, large wooden building. The Tolstoys still retain for their own use a minimum of the rooms in it, the rest being let-off to "workers". (As I write this in 1966, I am told that the whole house has now become a "National Museum" and the dining room—where I was entertained—remains now for ever set for dinner, with the thick blue and white china (which we used) and the other old table ornaments, the oil lamp, etc. I can see it still.)

'Count Sergei is the eldest son of old Leo Tolstoy, who only died a few years ago. He has a small government job, editing his father's manuscripts. When I turned over to the Countess the remains of the big white loaves that we had bought in the villages, they were already going green, like a gorgonzola cheese. She gasped with delight. "Give them to me" she said, "I can make use of that." She cut up the loaves, removed the green bits, added water and made it once again into dough, added yeast and baked such a loaf as Moscow had not seen for many a long day. But next day, when the loaf appeared, she and her husband entirely refused any share of it. That did make me feel bad but we could not move them.'

We were in Moscow about two weeks, trying to get passes etc. Rigg was trying to get permits for a re-settlement scheme for refugees in Siberia. Margaret Barber was looking for new nursing work for her ever-loved 'poor-ones'. Little had to go home urgently. Rigg asked me if I and R. R. Ball would go to the Polish Front, now peaceful, but reportedly thronged by refugees stopped by the German Army from returning home. Was there possibly some opportunity for us to help?

While we were trying to arrange this I was interviewed by the then British Ambassador, who found himself very isolated and without information. But when I realized he wanted to use me as a spy on my Russian friends I became dumb. At one office I met Comrade Sverdloff, one of the top Bolsheviki, and Commissar for Towns. He was helpful and anxious that I should go to the border at Orsha to see the situation there. R. R. Ball and myself got our passes and arranged to travel with a British student of music (so-called), whom we had met. He did not turn up for the train. Only months later did I find out the reason, when he was knighted for 'secret services in Russia'. We were better without such 'help'.

Getting on to a train for Orsha was again no joke. We were given permits for a 'sanitary train', which never started. Finally we got reserved places in a coach reserved for Party delegates, in unheard of luxury, with armed guards to keep out the mob!

At Orsha we got right down to the barbed wire set up by the German Army and saw their patrols on the far side. On the Russian side all was confusion and masses of refugees everywhere, all frustrated by the wire. Some Polish doctors were already operating a very

useful clinic but it seemed quite impossible for us to organize anything from so far away as England, and cut off as we were from home.

We therefore returned to Moscow. This time I met several
interesting people. There was Tchertkoff, Tolstoy's friend and
literary executor. He had had many years in England as an exile.
Olga Tolstoy took me to the Tretiakoff Gallery. I shall never forget
the picture by Ge (or Gay) of Christ and Pilate, 'What is Truth?'.
Christ is depicted as a fine but very puzzled peasant. I also met and
had a long conversation, in Russian, with Professor Sergei Bulgakoff,
who knew J. R. Mott and Ruth Rouse of the S.C.M. He was later
to settle in Paris. I also met a Mr Smernoff, then leading the small
Russian Christian Student Union.

Then at last I got my visa for home. I still had money for my
rail ticket to Archangelsk and Mourmansk in the far north, the only
way now open. On the train were many other Europeans taking the
same route home. I found that I was myself now classed as a refugee.
Arrived at Archangelsk we were all sent into a big empty building and
told to stay there. As no food was obtainable, a French warship
then in port, supplied us with emergency hard rations, and by virtue
of my uniform I was appointed, together with an ex-consul from
Tiflis, to distribute same.

Arrested

During many days of waiting I used my time to sketch some of the
unusual local church architecture. This led to my being arrested by a
passing soldier. I was taken to the court offices, searched and my
gold watch and documents confiscated. My baggage was also
searched. I asked to be allowed to speak to the British Consul. This
was allowed, but we might only speak in the Russian language
outside his front door. I soon realised that this consul was a man
whom they all greatly respected. Next morning I had to visit the
police again, when everything, even the disputed picture, was
returned to me. I think it helped that I was carrying some Tolstoyan
and S.C.M. literature, both of which were then acceptable to the
authorities. Also I had my Ikon and its certificate given by the
Liubimofka Soviet, which obviously guaranteed my genuineness. I
remember how the examining officer read it with much disgust
'Whatever sort of certificate will these people be giving next?' 'Kak
dadoot sviedetelsteff?' he remarked. I suppose it was not written
in his polished town Russian, but I am sure that its writers would
have been glad to know of its usefulness. I still keep it at the back
of my Ikon.

The old Orthodox Cathedral in Archangelsk is a strange building. A large wood building covered by oil paintings (in full technicolour), inside and out. Inside, the whole west wall is taken up by one huge picture, through which the main doors open. It represents the 'Last Judgment'. In one corner of the picture is a great red fire. Muscular hook-nosed devils are pulling and driving all sorts of people into it. One of these has a great club, knocking in an old man's head. Another has someone by the hair. A third is carrying off a girl in his arms, etc. In another part of the picture the devils are busy opening up graves in a cemetery, pulling bodies out and driving them to the fire. Beyond, several devils are swimming in a lake of brimstone, and quite enjoying it too. Presiding above all is God, the Ancient of Days. And there is still more to be seen. I think I have never seen such a terrible portrayal. Surely it is not Christian. Heavily jewelled Ikons abound in this Cathedral. There is a wooden cross made by Peter the Great himself. At the top of the main stairway outside are three old cannon, placed as though to fire at every approaching worshipper. I am glad that not all churches are like this one.

'On Saturday I was in a very different type of church at a "women's monastery" in the town. It was bright, worshipful and spotlessly clean . . . yet still orthodox.

'It was now July—mosquitoes were a plague everywhere, in the Arctic!'

We reach Mourmansk

After about two weeks in Archangelsk, two hundred of us 'refugees' were suddenly directed on to a small tramp steamer. I got a space in the empty hold, as did most others. We set off across the White Sea, already the haunt of active German submarines, escorted by two torpedo boats, one British, one Bolshevik. Half-way across, our Red escort suddenly sailed off south and the British one followed out of sight. What were they after, we wondered. We were disembarked at a small village port, Kandalashka, on the north-west shore of the White Sea, which was then already controlled by Allied Serbian troops. A short train journey brought us to Mourmansk on the Arctic Ocean, and more Allied occupying troops, including a British regiment. Mourmansk was then in the early stages of wartime construction as a port. Hills and valleys were being levelled off and huts were everywhere.

Very soon all Allied subjects of military age were called to Army Headquarters and told that we were soldiers under orders. I produced my Tribunal exemption certificate, only to get the reply that it was out of date! I still protested. Individual officers were quite nice but were puzzled as to what to do with me. My fellow refugees were just scared at the danger I was in, for this was an army in action at the Front. I was able to post a letter to the Friends at home, reporting and stating my position. This went via Consular mail.

My position was difficult. The Army would let me move nowhere. I told the officers that I was not trying to be difficult. I was willing to work for the local civilian population if so allowed, but I could not take military orders, but that I also felt that I should return to England to make my full report to the Friends Committee as per the terms of my exemption certificate.

While awaiting developments I met a number of people, among them an American chaplain, who lent me Fosdick's new book, *The Challenge of the Present Crisis*, a profoundly Christian book, in which he admits that the Quaker position is more ideal than his own, but in which he defends the position of the Christian who feels he must join up. . . . I was almost convinced that I was perhaps too self-opinionated. Then one day I lay in my bunk in the crowded noisy barrack where we were all housed, and read right through St. Matthew's Gospel at one reading. At the end of that I was quite sure of what I ought to do. I could make no compromise . . . but we are often so weak. . . . Apart from these conflicts, I was kept busy at Mourmansk attending to all my fellow refugees as patients, distributing rations, vaccinating, etc. I had to decide who would be on the ration list for tinned milk, etc. We had about 150 English refugees, men, women and children, in our hut.

Eventually a telegram arrived at the Consul's office from Miss Ruth Fry of the F.W.V.R.C. office in London, saying she was approaching the Foreign Office in London to O.K. my passage home. I took this with me on my next visit to the camp. The officer on duty showed it to his colonel, who at once marked my passport 'O.K. for U.K.' I was free to go home.

Next day a large Cunard liner arrived in Mourmansk with more troops. We refugees were put on board the empty liner. It was August 4th, 1918. An erratic course to avoid submarine attention brought us one fine day into port. We were at Lerwick. Out to sea again, and when we again saw land we had no idea where we were. We were landing at Newcastle-on-Tyne! My days in Russia were over.

CHAPTER FIVE

To Work in Hunan

AMONGST all the post-war confusion of the last months of 1919, it was not until January 1920 that the way opened and passports were obtained by the Methodist Missionary Society for us to go to China, and even then the only passages obtainable were on an old Austrian boat sailing under the Italian flag from Venice, the S.S. 'Pilsna'. We were a large party of missionaries and children led by the Rev. E. C. Cooper, an 'old China hand'. We had a nightmare trip across post-war Europe with all our heavy baggage, meeting a national railway strike in Italy. and only getting on board with minutes to spare, but all complete, as the ship sailed.

But new adventures were not far away. As the good ship 'Pilsna' weighed anchor she at once listed to one side, about 25 degrees and she remained like that until we reached Port Said! There she decided to change sides, and listed the opposite way. I believe people on the bund thought she was going to turn right over. After that the Captain took on sand ballast and we were more normal. Our crew was all Communist and occupied the third class rooms. To add to my worries, after leaving Venice, Mary had gone down with a high fever (influenza pneumonia). She was breast feeding baby Christine. The ship could provide no invalid foods for her or the baby, but she bravely continued the feeding, until at Port Said I was able to buy powdered milk. It was a joy as we sailed on south to see her gradually recovering. By Colombo all was well.

At Hong Kong we were met by Mary's sister, Phyllis Gibson, then working with her husband in the English Presbyterian Mission at Swatow, and taken by coasting vessel to her home for a few days. Then north again to Shanghai and on by Yangtse river steamer to Hankow. A short stay, meeting some of the pioneers of our mission and on by another steamer to Changsha in Hunan, then still a Treaty Port. Our Chairman, Rev. G. G. Warren, was on the landing among a noisy crowd of coolies to greet us. We were not alone. 'Others have laboured. Ye have entered into their labours.' We were part of a team.

The great city gates were locked but Mr Warren beckoned us to follow him. He walked right up to the locked gates, pulled from his pocket a small official token, pushed it under the gates and called to the guards to open. At once the big old gates were flung open, and we passed into the city. Of that great missionary pioneer, G. G. Warren,

47

I have written more elsewhere.

We now spent three months in Changsha, doing language study, also helping to entertain for a week the embryo Synod of the Hunan Methodist Church. During the hot weather we were sent down river to the hill resort of Kuling, there to continue with our teacher, old Mr Yang. It was September 1920 when we finally reached Paoking, later renamed Shaoyang, which was to be our other home for the next thirty years.

Overland to Paoking

What a journey! Something quite outside any tourist programme. Going to Paoking were the Stanfield family with their baby, and Mary and I, with six-months-old Christine. Only Mr Stanfield had been over the road before. It was usually a five day trip, four nights on the road, 150 miles. The first thirty miles was by river to Siangtan on an extremely overcrowded steam launch, no regulations about overcrowding. You got on if you could find standing room—and that was that.

Arrived at Siangtan, we went to an inn which was a contact point for Paoking coolies. As we were moving up country to live we had with us all our household equipment, bedding, crockery, baby-linen and bath, kitchen utensils, food stores, etc. All had to be carried by the coolies and it had to be parcelled out amongst them, so that each man got the regulation weight of about 100 pounds divided into two bundles of 50 pounds each. Undividable loads, like cabin trunks, needed two men each. What a noise and a hubbub while all this was sorted out. It was dusk before we got away. We then found out that we were travelling behind a train of thirty loaded coolies. We ourselves, each had a sedan chair carried by two men. Babes were crying, dogs barking and every coolie protesting about something or other. After only two or three miles it got dark and we stopped at a wayside inn. No coolie travels in the dark.

For us the inn was another problem. These country inns are all the same. A rough mud wall, a very rough and dusty mud floor and the main room of the inn wide open on to the road. Somewhere at the back is usually one small dark and dirty bedroom, often next to the pigsty, for guests who preferred privacy. The wooden beds have rough straw mattresses and mosquito curtains that are never washed, and they are well stocked with what Mark Tapley (himself an inn-keeper in old England) called 'Wampires'. Arrived at an inn, we had to unpack our bedding, cover the existing mattress with a large local oiled sheet (to restrain invaders from below), put up our mosquito nets (to keep off those that fly by night or drop from the rafters), and make our beds. Meanwhile the babes had to be bathed and fed and put into their travelling cots. Then only could we get to our own meal, either of rice or of what we had brought with us, and so tumble off to sleep.

Next morning the coolies would want to start at dawn. We had to be up and packed and fed before daylight and a hurried prayer too. And so we were off again for another thirty miles till at dusk we again turned in for the night.

Yes, this was the sort of routine with which Mary found she had to cope. So very different from life at home, and always more difficult when travelling with a small family. But she just carried on so wonderfully.

The sedan chairs in use in Hunan are a light bamboo frame slung from two long bamboo poles, carried on the men's shoulders. They usually have a cover of cloth to keep off sun or rain. Sanitation at the inns is usually an open pit at the back of the inn, with loose boards over it to stand on and a rough roof. This is all part of the Chinese farmer's method of returning all manure to the fields as fertilizer, a most praiseworthy economic process, but to one used to the usual 'mod. con.' benefits of 'civilization', rather a trial.

Paoking

'Paoking', meaning 'Precious Felicity', was the Imperial name for our city. 'Shaoyang', meaning 'Town-on-the-left-bank-of-the-Shao-River', was an older name, which again came into use during Revolutionary days. When we arrived in September 1920 it was still a sleepy old place with its stone wall, built long before Christ. Every night its gates were shut to keep out bandits. Its streets were dark and very narrow; no room for cars or carts; everywhere were stone steps, up and down. All traffic had to come and go carried by men. Passengers were carried in sedan chairs: all shops open to the street: no glass fronts. Everyone had time to spare and long bargaining was the rule. Only foolish and rich foreigners pay the first price asked.

The countryside is beautiful and prosperous. There are high mountains and large tracts of level, well-watered plains. The land often produces two main crops a year. Rice is always a rich-yielding crop. It demands large numbers of cultivators, first to make and level the irrigated fields and prepare them for use. Every rice plant must be planted out by hand into the prepared flooded fields. Water levels must be daily watched and adjusted. Later the crop must be cut,

49

carried and threshed by hand. Through the centuries every tiny bit of hillside that can be levelled and where water can be had, has been brought under rice crop. New methods are not easy to introduce into this cycle of man and nature. Perhaps fifty per cent of the land in the Paoking area consists of beautiful limestone hills, rising to over 3,000 feet above steep green valleys. Bamboos and bushes, azaleas, roses, rhododendrons and forsythias flourish. In the hills are found antimony, silver, molybdenum, sulphur, gypsum, iron and coal in quantity. This latter is still mined in the old way by digging a hole in a field and then walking down to get it. Some of these mines are thirty or forty feet deep, without any machinery and only naked lights, if any.

Paoking is also a busy trading centre. Fur traders from the hills bring in the skins for sale. You can buy a 'tiger' any day, or skins of the greatly prized Chinese otter. There is a sizable cast-iron and hand forge iron industry. Sugar cane is grown and made into a crude brown sugar. Carving on bamboo is an esteemed local skill. The building of wooden junks thrives. Softwood is built into large boats, which are filled with coal, taken down the rapids and sold, both wood and coal, in Hankow. Many of these unwieldy craft are lost on the rapids of the River Tzu, but still it pays handsomely. These boats never come back. But there is also a fleet of better, hardwood junks which regularly do the trip both ways.

Roads

In those days in Hunan the only roads were still the ancient, barrow footpaths, three or four feet wide, paved with large limestone slabs and worn to a polish by the straw sandals of countless generations of Chinese coolies. (The word for coolie or 'ku-li' in Chinese means 'Bitter Strength' or perhaps 'Sweating Labour'.) They will carry a load of one hundredweight or more for thirty miles a day, day after day. As one of these old roads approaches a town there is often a fine stone archway built across the road. These may be memorials to some virtuous widow or some past event.

Motor roads came later. The first road into Paoking from Siangtan was actually built as a Famine Relief Project, and was the direct result of a letter which I wrote to the United Relief Committee at Changsha in 1924, urging the value of 'real work' as relief, and the need of this route in particular. After that was completed, new style roads began to multiply as a direct Government enterprise.

Opium

Opium was then freely on sale. Poppies grew everywhere, even

50

directly outside our own front door, despite solemn treaty obliga-
tions. These were still the days of the War Lords, each of whom kept
his private army, and they fought their wars round the countryside
as one waxed and another waned. But even these wars were politely
waged and the victor was usually careful to leave a convenient way
of escape for a defeated rival. There was no civil service. Each new
ruler brought along his own train of family hangers-on, who were
expected to support themselves by graft and incompetence. The
common people suffered in silence.

The People

The people of Paoking, being Hunanese, are proud and independent. They are small of stature but lively and intelligent. They have
always provided a very high proportion of China's leaders. Almost
every town in Hunan has its own dialect, some very broad, due it is
said, to whole populations having been introduced en bloc, after
old and forgotten wars. Naturally materialist or Confucianist in
their thinking, superstition was not far under the surface as the
following shows:

In 1902, the town magistrate (the local ruler) was a certain Mr
Ho Ching-Sheng, a fine old-style patriot. The very first telegraph
line from Changsha to Paoking was then being planned. With
foreign help the provincial governor had ordered work to proceed.
Mr Ho opposed the idea and was perhaps suspected of aiming to
support his views by force. The Provincial Governor called him to
come to Changsha for a conference. He complied, but at the very
border of his county area he was met by a squad of the Governor's
troops and beheaded on the spot. And so the telegraph came to
Paoking.

Not many years later, during our own early years in the district,
we found that this same Mr Ho, under his posthumous name of
Ho Lieh-Shih (the Victorious Scholar) had been elevated to become
a god in many local temples. I myself saw one of these new idols
being carved and later being worshipped. It stands now among many
other gods. Prayer made to Ho Lieh-Shih is said to be very effective.

In those early days, and even throughout our stay in Hunan we
found that justice was rough. Mercy, pity and love were often at a
discount. On one occasion, walking along the narrow, crowded
streets, I met a party of Chinese soldiers hurrying along. In the
midst of them was a man bound and led by a rope. He was on
his way to be executed just outside the city walls. I know not what
was his offence. It might even have been political. But I can never

51

forget his pale, shocked face with its look of hopeless horror, helpless and silent, as he struggled to keep up with his captors. Is that what crucifixion meant?

We begin work—September 1920
At Paoking on the mission compound, beside the chapel, we found a small building, erected by Doctor Pell, but cramped and quite insufficient for regular hospital work. There were several large boxes of hospital equipment, packed and stored since 1912. As we opened the boxes, blankets literally fell to pieces due to mould and decay over eight years. But ten strong iron beds, made by Warrington Wire Rope Works were like new, and continued in use for the next thirty years. We also discovered Doctor Pell's original name plate advertising the 'Hospital of Universal Love' (Pu-Ai-I-Yuan) and we used that as our title.

My chief job for the next two years was language study, every morning, with my old teacher, Mr Yang Hung-Wu. By midday, when my brain had begun to reel, I was able to start a small daily clinic with the aid of an interpreter, often Mrs Stanfield. I also had the help of a Chinese trainèd male nurse from Hankow, Mr Tang Ta-Chi.

Our dispensary occupied two small rooms next to the chapel. Any equipment needed had to come all the way from England, also medicines. For a long time we could not get bottles and had to ask patients to bring their own. The variety of bottles that turned up was amazing. For ointments we were able to get a local tinsmith to make very useful little tins from old paraffin cans.

There was no immediate crowd of patients. Just a few dared to come to consult this foreigner. To begin with we charged a small fee to those who could pay, on the principle that the Chinese is a good businessman, and if he gets something for nothing he knows just how much that is worth, but if he pays he will use his medicine carefully. Poor patients were always treated free. Numbers increased but slowly.

After a year or two we cautiously began to admit one or two in-patients. This meant organizing a Chinese kitchen in an odd corner and engaging a cook and a coolie. I was also happy when Doctor Hadden of Yungchow was able to send me another boy who had had some experience in the new hospital at Yungchow. His name was Dang Pang Mei. He became a most useful man and stayed with us for many years.

Finding a site

During the war years, and after, a small mission fund had been accumulating for medical work in Shaoyang (to avoid confusion, from now on I will use the new name instead of Paoking). Stanfield and I were therefore instructed to look out for any possible land or site suitable for an entirely new hospital. Rented premises seem impossible under existing Chinese law and custom. Such enquiries took time. Eventually, an old builder, Mr Yang, was able to get the offer of a small plot, perhaps two and a quarter acres, immediately outside the city on the main path to the east country. To us it had an additional advantage in that it had a back exit opening on to a vacant hill cemetery, only fifty yards from the back of the chapel compound. The land was owned by four families, but a bargain was struck. They all agreed to sell. The necessary feast was given, documents exchanged, and just before the Chinese New Year the cash was paid over in hard silver dollars. Perhaps the need of every Chinese for ready money at that season helped. God had given us a place in Shaoyang.

On the site were two small but usable farmhouses built of mud brick. The site was in part hillside, with a lower level area devoted to rice cultivation, all open and rather fragmented. On this open land our first need was for a compound wall if we were to have a unified institution to house nurses and the like, in a land where police supervision was still at a minimum. Our wall was to be of hard pounded earth and lime with a tile roof. It cost us over £100, a big sum in those days, but it paid for itself again and again in the days of the War Lords and their disorderly armies. We could shut our doors and carry on.

Our next need was a doctor's bungalow on the new site. It was the ambition of Mary and myself that our new home should be useful, yet modest and inexpensive, suitable alike for European and Chinese staff. Many of the earlier mission houses seemed too large and out of place in their context, having been built at a time when English money exchange rates made them seem cheap to those who sent the money. We therefore deliberately chose sun-dried mud brick for the house walls, covered with white lime plaster. This makes an admirable finish. There were also other economies, and in the end our new home only cost 2,700 Mexican dollars or about £300.

Work starts on the Hospital Building

This was to be our Out-Patients Department. I had been able to borrow a surveyor's compass and so I could map out the land and prepare plans on paper. These had to go first to the Hunan Methodist Synod and then to the Mission in London before funds could be had. I was not able to find any local contractors to undertake the work, so I had to make my own estimates of quantities and prices. I could, however, get good local bricklayers and carpenters who could work from day to day to my own drawings. I therefore now found myself the clerk of works as well as architect, paymaster, medical expert and local preacher, etc., etc.

But at this point I will lay down my own pen and let Mary tell in her own words what she saw going on, as I have an old letter of hers written at this period:

'Before any work could be done the Doctor had to make an accurate map of both the old chapel compound and the new site. Then from his brain he began to evolve the new hospital. Night after night he worked using all that he knew of hospitals at home, or of those already seen in China. Gradually the hospital took shape, also homes for Doctor and the expected Matron. After approval of the plans, materials had to be gathered together for the buildings.

'1921 was a year of severe famine in Hunan, so building materials could be had cheaply. But famine prices for rice were soon making high wages a necessity. No contractors could be found, but local bricklayers and carpenters are skilled. Chinese styles are to be used where possible. Great blocks of limestone were used for the foundation. One buys these stones at so much a piece to a minimum standard size and the price includes trenching to specified depth and the placing of the stones in position by the stone-masons. Burnt bricks had to be made to order. Wood was required. For this the Doctor and his helper, a Chinese preacher and ex-carpenter, Mr Tseng by name went down to the Tzu River to look for passing rafts of logs. Having bargained for three rafts of well-seasoned Chinese red pine (*cunninghamia*) which is reputed to resist attack by white ants, coolies had to be found to carry all the whole logs over a mile from wharf to hospital site. Chinese burnt bricks and curved tiles had also to be ordered months in advance, thousands and thousands of them.

'At last, building began. It was really exciting to watch things grow. Gradually the wall crept round until the whole area was enclosed. Then the bungalow began to rise and we would walk around on the floor beams and plan what to do with this corner or that room...

'It fills me with wonder that every little detail, almost to each nail, has had to pass through the Doctor's hands. All the accounts have to be passed by him and he has to be constantly on the watch to see that things are done rightly. The help of Mr Tseng has been invaluable. He has acted as foreman, but even he is not as particular as the Doctor about details. For Chinese, he seemed to think, anything was good enough, and as for lavatory arrangements—well the foreigner is quite mad!

'At the beginning of October 1923 we were able to move into our new home; and not long after that all the hospital work moved over the hill into its new quarters. The formal opening took place a few weeks later when the City Magistrate himself attended and was elaborately entertained with his colleagues to a grand feast which included three sucking pigs in the old style. Rev. W. W. Gibson was also with us. He is the one man whose work, alone for so many years, has made it all possible.

'Among the few in-patients moved into the new premises was one dangerously ill woman, who had been shot by brigands. They had entered her house and asked for money; as she had none they shot her in the abdomen and the child she was nursing was wounded in the foot. She had been brought to us very ill with multiple perforation of the intestines. Doctor Pearson operated with little hope of success (we had no such thing as penicillin then) but she did recover after a long time of uncertainty. The child was also in hospital and its father was with them almost continuously. They were simple country people and very grateful for everything. We are trying to keep in touch with them after their return home. . .'

A Problem of Thieves

How does one deal with thieving or pilfering in a country where a modern police force is either non-existent or hopelessly corrupt or tyrannical? Soon after we started our first building operations in Shaoyang we had to store quite a lot of building materials on the new site. We put a watchman on the site to look after things. One day not long afterwards, I received a sudden alarm call. . . 'Come at once, the watchman is beating up a thief whom he has caught redhanded.' I went along, saw what was happening, stopped the beating and escorted the thief to my house near the chapel. We then searched the thief—and found only a few oddments, including a strychnine bean (which might be used to silence troublesome dogs). The man was a wretched, poorly-clad coolie. I did not want to hand him over to the police.

I decided first to give him a good meal of rice and vegetables, take his finger-prints, and then, as it was late in the day, we locked him up in the cellar—not a very secure place—and gave him a rug for the night. There he stayed till next day. Next morning we unlocked the door, returned his sundries to him and took him to the back door and told him to go. But he at first declined to go. Suddenly he realised that we really meant it and bolted at the double. Having reached a safe distance, he stopped, turned round, bowed to us an elaborate gesture of thanks and was gone. We never had any more trouble on his lines. Did he belong to a thieves' guild?

On another occasion perhaps even earlier, one night Mary and I both heard a persistent scraping noise near our bedroom window and the occasional sound of something solid falling. The compound outside wall was close to. I got up but could see nothing with my torch. When the noise continued I roused our cook and together we opened the back gate of the compound. We soon found the cause. A thief had been actually digging a hole through the brick wall ten feet from our room, but so far only the outer layer of bricks had been removed. He had made his get-away in good time and did not return.

CHAPTER SIX

The New Hospital—Destroyed by Flood

BUILT on a site of just two and a quarter acres on the eastern fringe of the city, the new Hospital was essentially a group of low buildings, some of them two-storied. To begin with, we had used mud-dried brick, but after the floods we used a local grey coloured burnt brick. The general lay-out can be seen in the printed plan. When finally completed in 1943 we could boast of 120 beds in four wards and a few private rooms, but we only attained these numbers after many years of work. Our other equipment included a busy Out-Patient Department able to accommodate three doctors working at the same time. Waiting hall, operation theatre, X-ray rooms, office, kitchen, laundry, drug dispensary, laboratory, bath-house, isolation wards, maternity department, and a School-of-Nursing building with accommodation for fifty girls in training. Also seven homes for married staff, mortuary, and even our own dairy, staffed by a small herd of Jerseys and Ayrshires.

At the centre of it all was our small Hospital Chapel, built like an old Chinese temple with curving upturned roof ends. It had a terminal cross at each end, and the whole front facing the hospital, was formed of the traditional carved wood doors, surmounted by large black and gold Chinese inscriptions, quoting the gospels: 'With all your soul, all your mind, all your heart, all your strength.' Inside, at each side of the reading desk hung rhymed Chinese texts: (1) 'He that endureth to the end shall be saved' and (2) 'The humble man when he be raised has honour'. A carved reading desk showed a gold cross, with lotus flowers growing up from the mud (Purity growing amongst filth) and the Spirit descending in the form of two flying birds.

Somewhat similar was the altar table in our Shaoyang Church, but for that I took a Chinese picture of the Last Supper by the artist Mrs Hsu. I transferred and enlarged the picture in pencil on to a prepared piece of camphor wood; this then was beautifully carved in relief by a local wood-worker and finished with the best lacquer.

This hospital chapel was always a thing very near my heart. It was planned to stand at the very centre of the compound and of all our work. It was used for daily morning prayers and was also a social centre for all the staff.

The first part of the buildings to be completed was the Out-Patient block. This was planned as a twin O.P.D., one side for men and one for women, because senior missionaries at that time believed that we could never get shy secluded countrywomen to attend at a hospital for men. As things worked out, however, the women's side soon came into urgent use as ward accommodation. We found no difficulty at all in running one clinic for both men and women, and especially so when we had women nurses. In this we never looked back.

The O.P.D., our largest building, was not expensive. Even in those early days, about 1923, it cost us only a bare £1,000 of mission money.

Adaptations

In all the work of building I kept my eyes open for any local materials which might be used, rather than buy imported stuff. Local products were always much cheaper.

For instance, our sterilizers were heated on Chinese-style coal stoves. These looked black but they gave the needed heat and the boiling water. In the absence of running water, surgical handwashing had to be done in sterilized enamel bowls, sterilized by burning native spirit in them. Chinese teapots found many uses, especially as feeders and for washing sore eyes. Wooden buckets were in constant use. The narrow bamboo beds in use everywhere in Hunan became excellent stretchers if two bamboo poles were lashed alongside. A larger pressure sterilizer was heated over a special charcoal burner.

Our carpenters produced excellent furniture made from the local camphor wood. They even made me a comfortable armchair copied from a current advertisement in a stray volume of *Punch*. A very effective operating table was produced in camphor wood with brass hinges and fittings, made to my drawings by the local old-style brass-smith. It was based on one which had been previously made for Doctor Hadden at Yungchow. It was finished in locally grown red-brown 'chi' or lacquer which gave it an entirely waterproof polished surface, impervious even to solvents like chloroform, and its joints could do almost anything demanded of a modern operating table. It was still in regular use to the end of my days in Shaoyang.

All hospital windows, as also in our own home, were screened against flies and mosquitoes with strong locally woven hemp net, which was very satisfactory and cheap as it was in daily use in all the villages as a mosquito screening for their beds.

When the builders got to work on some curved roof porches which I had asked for in my plans, they adorned them with a most wonderful array of stucco dragons and phoenix-birds disporting themselves thereon. These men were natural artists and only asked to be allowed a few more hours on the job to produce virtuoso results. For painting the woodwork we needed no expensive imported paints. 'Tung oil' or 'wood oil' is grown locally and when boiled gives an excellent finish. In fact it is extensively exported to U.S.A. to help their paint industry.

Water Supply

Lack of any possibility of running water was a headache. I find that doctors who have never had to work under such a handicap find it hard to understand how we managed. For all the work of a modern hospital was undertaken, even major operations like Caesarians, laparatomies, or even cataracts, etc. It was a matter of going back to first principles and working out what could be done with materials at hand and in our limited financial circumstances. And our methods gave results. On more than one occasion I was quite happy to submit myself for operation by a colleague in our own theatre, with the best results.

Our actual water sources when we started were either from the large Shao River, 500 yards away, or from an unreliable public well only fifty yards from our gate. All water needed had to be carried in buckets. Both these sources must have been badly contaminated by sewage, so all drinking water had to be boiled.

A special gift from my brother Victor, then a general practitioner in Cheshire, was earmarked to dig a new well on our own land. Local stonemasons undertook to dig it and we found water, though not nearly enough for all our needs. They had to dig down for twenty-five feet through soft yellow clay. It was a dangerous job due to falling clay but they got it done and well lined with limestone blocks. I rounded it off by buying and installing a small valve-pump for hand working. Alas, our untrained coolies were always getting into trouble with the pump. It was always going wrong and I was the only person who could do any repairs, there were no local engineers of any sort in those days. These repairs took up so much of my time, which I could ill afford, that in the end I gave up. I removed the pump and in its place put over the top of the well a large dressed limestone slab, with a carved hole in its raised centre, too small to admit anything but a specially constructed bucket, and able to drain away all surface water. This was much more useful than the expensive pump and would last for ever!

Running tap water was long planned by the town authorities, and was probably installed soon after we left in 1951.

59

Unexpected Hazards—War

The years of the growth and development of the hospital were most of them years of continuous and recurrent civil wars and disturbances. On three occasions—or was it four? Mary and I and the family had to pack up and depart almost overnight. Once a battle was fought literally over our heads, two armies faced each other across the valley in which the hospital lay, and were shooting at each other. We had to lie behind our mud walls to avoid flying bullets. At the end of the day, when the armies decided to go elsewhere, we crept out and our staff got busy picking up the wounded left on the fields around us.

Floods

It was June 1924. We had completed our first year's work in the new hospital, when an unexpected hazard struck. I had to go down to Changsha to attend the annual Synod, and then on to join the family who were in Kuling mountain resort in Kiangsi, to get away from the heat of summer. This time I chose the route via Hengyang, normally a three days march and then by boat down the Siang River.

As I left Shaoyang the rain started. It really did rain—tropical rain—without stopping, all the time. Towards evening the second day, we found our road blocked by deep water right across the limestone path. Water still rising. Should we—could we—turn back? As I hesitated I saw a small sampan (rowing boat) tethered nearby, its owner crouching down in it, trying to keep dry. A short chat and an offer of a fair price and he agreed to let myself and my three coolies on board. A military officer, also stranded, added himself to the company. The boatman agreed to deliver me to Hengyang and off we went.

Over fields and hedges, over hill and dale. Soon we came to a village, still above water, but its big stone bridge over the river stood isolated like an island above the floods, the waters swirling round it. We disembarked our officer. Then our boatman navigated us carefully round the bridge, and as it was getting dark, he anchored for the night in an area of rice fields. After a simple supper I spread my bed for the night and the men also turned in. I took the opportunity to read aloud a few verses from the gospels and spoke very simply of the God that the Christians worship.

Half-way through the night I was awakened by the boat rocking violently and by the boatman shouting to his son. We had lost our anchor and were drifting out of control, down the torrent, in the dark.

60

Just as dawn broke I suddenly realised we were rushing broadside on to another isolated stone bridge. As we got nearer there seemed to be just about one foot of space under the main arch. Skilled boatmanship might just perhaps manage to let us shoot through it if we lay flat and let the tent above us go. I had to leave it to the experts. Somehow they managed to pull the boat up broadside on to one of the piers. There we stuck, the boat held as in a vice by the rush of water against the bridge. We were unable to move any way, and there we stayed till daylight, nothing but rushing water round us, our little cockleshell quietly riding the waves. But the rain had stopped. As it got light the boatman found that he could climb up on to the bridge and look around and from that vantage point he was able to edge the boat round one end of the island bridge and into calmer waters, and so on to Hengyang. The only comment that this pagan boatman made was: 'That God of yours must be a good one to bring us out of this!'

As we passed that day through the drowned countryside we saw many families sitting on the roofs of their homes, but he refused all my suggestions to try to do something for them, taking me straight down river to my destination.

I arrived in Changsha having to wade carefully through town streets three feet deep in the filthiest muddy water imaginable. Synod was in session and the younger missionaries were enjoying themselves making and navigating rafts to travel across the garden and into town. A few days later I continued down the Yangtse to Kuling. There I was met at the hilltop by a very worried wife and friends. They had got a message from Mr Tang Ta-Chi in Shaoyang, to say that our new hospital had just disappeared in the floods! And would I please return at once? Next day therefore, I started my return trip of eight or nine days to Shaoyang.

Back at Hospital

What a sight of destruction met my eyes! The Tzu River had risen overnight almost fifty feet above its normal height, sweeping away even the largest bridges and leaving ruin everywhere. Afterwards, someone told me that there had once been a similar flood about 350 years ago in the records. We had anticipated nothing of the sort. The dried mud bricks which we had used just melted away, but the main roof which was largely supported on a wooden framework, remained intact. Wooden floors just floated around and furniture was every where. When the waters receded everything was covered inches deep in mud. The old farm houses which we were using, and which

61

had been there many years, both completely collapsed. Everywhere was chaos. The staff had already moved remaining in-patients up into my own house above flood level. What could we do?

I had my camera with me so I at once took a few pictures, got them developed and sent them with a description of the disaster to the Mission in London. Help was then soon made available, while we on the spot got busy to clear up some of the worst of the mess and to plan for reconstruction. Very soon a daily out-patient clinic was functioning under the roof, but in rooms without walls.

The following winter was one of re-planning and re-building. This time using burnt brick for everything anywhere near flood level. Entirely new houses were needed for staff, and for kitchen and laundry.

A Second Flood

Years later, in June 1949, a similar flood struck. This time Mary and myself were both on the spot and saw it all happen. The River Tzu after leaving Shaoyang, passes through some very narrow, deep gorges in the mountains and with heavy rain these gorges just cannot take all the water, which then backs up and makes the whole area one huge lake.

Mary has left her description of events in 1949:

'We have been having a good deal of rain for weeks past, which made the days pleasantly cool. Then on Sunday, 5th June, 1949, the heat increased, clouds threatened and thunder muttered. That night we got little sleep owing to the incessant thunder and lightning and torrential rain. Next day, Monday, the river was an awesome sight as it swept under the high bridge. No boats were attempting to cross. We were told that one boat had been swept from its moorings and crashed against the piers with loss of life. That was something to talk about, but nothing compared with what was to follow. Rain continued to fall and by Tuesday afternoon many city streets were awash. Soon the river was actually flowing over the high bridge roadway itself and was still rising. Of course, by now vast areas of countryside were hopelessly under water in all directions.

'Our hospital stands in a little side valley, 500 yards from the main stream of the River Shao. On Tuesday afternoon from the hill at the back of the hospital, we could see people having to abandon their little mud houses, and boatmen doing a good trade bargaining for rescue work or removals. Before dark that day the rain had stopped, but the water continued to rise and was beginning to creep into the hospital compound.

'At once work was begun to evacuate our lowest-lying buildings, moving patients and goods uphill out of danger. Before going to bed Doctor Pearson arranged for an alarm bell to be sounded if the water continued to rise. The gong rang at 11 p.m. and again at 1.30 a.m. No one slept that night. The whole staff worked valiantly and everything of value was methodically moved to a place of safety. One ward was evacuated into the hospital Chapel, Medical Superintendent and Matron directing and sharing in the work.

'The night was calm and still and a bright moon shining. In such a setting it seemed all the more tragic to hear the rumble and crash of falling houses as the water turned their sun-dried mud bricks into soft mud. Houses of burnt brick or of wood were in less danger, so this time patients on our first floor wards felt no alarm.

'Daylight came, and the sullen looking water continued to creep up the steps, inch by inch. Next therefore, the Women's Ward and the Maternity Block had to be evacuated, the latter into the Matron's own home. All was done smoothly and efficiently without a grumble from anyone. It was hard work with no chance to rest and the food supply was very sketchy. The main kitchen was used until the water put the fires out. After that it was cook where you can ...

'The water reached its highest level on Wednesday midday, at which time the water was eight feet deep at the hospital main gate, and the river must have been over fifty feet above its normal level. That same evening the water began to retreat, and next day the staff started to clear up the mess. Rooms which had stood in several feet of water were soon looking spick and span again. Unhappily, our new electric generator which provided our lighting and X-ray had been overtaken by the water. It was very heavy; while the water was rising we had succeeded in loosening it from its concrete bed and jacking it up on bricks but we could not get it high enough to escape that last few feet of rise, when the floods had gone it just refused to work and in the disturbed political conditions then obtaining, we never found anyone with sufficient skill to put it right. It was our greatest loss.

'Once again it was the poorest of the people who suffered most and whose homes were swept away. One riverside village just disappeared with its 2,000 people ...'

Apart from keeping the hospital running, it is good to record that this time the local church, under minister Deng, got busy: housing homeless people in the church and subscribing money to buy rice, to make rice-gruel to help feed the many camped on higher ground all round. Unhappily, political tensions and the expected Red invasion made any larger schemes impossible.

CHAPTER SEVEN

Daily Chores

THROUGH the years the daily work of the hospital increased so that we had a regular O.P.D. Clinic of from 100 to 200 cases each morning on six days of the week. We were the only modern hospital in a scattered population of perhaps 3,000,000 people in Shaoyang and all its surrounding counties. Patients with almost every possible disease were to be seen daily. Surgical conditions predominated. Every person with a wound would come to us, whereas people suffering from fevers and the like, still had faith in the old style drugs and the 'Lei-ko' or 'Internal Disease' healers. These patients tended to come only in their last extremity.

Tuberculosis in all forms was always prominent, infection spreading easily in closely crowded houses and among people often under-nourished. As a touring Yugoslav professor of the League of Nations once said to me of this 'Eet ees an ekonomik problem'. He was right, for so often we saw these cases improve rapidly while in hospital, only to relapse as soon as they got home again. College students in particular were terrified of T.B. So many of their number contracted it when subject to the stress of their studies.

Typhoid was always with us. In those days it needed a long course of ward treatment and skilled nursing, and many were our disappointments when a patient, just turning the corner, was whisked away by anxious relatives almost certainly to die at home. Old custom demanded that if there was any possibility of death, the patient MUST die in his own home family.

Typhus and Relapsing Fever appeared sporadically, and especially in the local prison, the old 'Prison Fever'. When this got too bad the authorities several times asked us to visit the prisoners inside, where the presence of bed bugs, the recognized vector of the disease, was only too easy to see. On these visits we were often accompanied by the Chinese minister who held a service for the inmates. They (the prisoners) were all accommodated in large dormitories sleeping in two-layer wooden bunks. It was always a strange feeling going through those double-locked wooden doors and meeting such a sad collection of humanity inside.

Smallpox was endemic and vaccination campaigns were often organized.

Measles was also frequent, and very fatal when it attacked the small devitaminized children.

Gold-mounted ikon presented to the Author by the Liubimofka Village Soviet, 1918. A translation of the accompanying official document reads:

'Much esteemed Giorgi Karlovitch (George, son of Charles),

We the undersigned citizens of Liubimofka Village of the Liubimofka District of the Buzuluk Division of the Samara Province, herewith bring to you our truest thanks for the warm and heartfelt relationship which you, *Comrade Pearson*, showed to our poorest people in that you did not spare your strength, and would be hindered by nothing, that you might show them every assistance. Many of us have seen the happy life of those saved from death, when to others there seemed to be nothing but death before them. You of your kindness and effort gave them the needed help and stilled their fears.

As a sign of our thankfulness, accept from us a real *Russian thank you*. We give you today a sacred picture of the Saviour, may it guard you in all future movements for the relief of suffering or disease.

March 23, 1918.

The above thanks of the Liubimofka Village Soviet of Peasants Deputies is certified with the Village Seal—

(Signed) *Chairman*: SKLAROFF
Secretary: NEEKULIN'

Stone
Memorial Arch
standing across
the old main road
into Paoking, 1920

Boats on the River Shao, Shaoyang

Other things frequently seen were enteritis, dysentery, both amoeba and bacilliary types; cholera epidemics appeared from time to time; leprosy existed in certain villages. Malaria and hookworm were frequent. On the latter, Doctor C. T. Yang and I did some research, publishing an article in the Chinese Medical Journal, demonstrating the high percentage of infected cases especially amongst the men of farming families. Shaoyang had not previously been known as a hookworm area.

We saw some severe epidemics of cerebro-spinal meningitis of the meningococcal type. During one of these epidemics, the local authority asked me to go out into the country to investigate and see what might be done, as so many people were dying. In a tour of several days we found many ill and dying people, some of whom we were able to help with injections and Sulpha drugs. We duly reported to the Magistrates' office.

And of course, there were all the more usual day-to-day diseases— heart disease, cancer cases of all sorts, a few still operable. Cases of syphilis and gonorrhoea were frequent, with an insistent demand for the then treatment by injections of Neo-salvarsan (914). Bronchitis influenza, not to mention skin diseases. These filled in our days.

Surgically we had to be prepared for anything that could possibly come within the scope of our small team of one, or possibly two, doctors. We had a good selection of surgical instruments at hand, with our nurses trained in the administration of simple Open Ether or 'CE' mixture. Spinal anaesthesia was very useful for many cases, and 'local' often suitable. Cases treated included wounds and fractures of every kind, especially gunshot wounds. We were glad of our X-ray in later years. Stone in bladder was frequent. Strangulated hernias, appendicitis, huge ovarian cysts, etc. etc.

Eye diseases were always prominent, often forming twenty-five per cent of a morning's clinic. Trachoma and its sequellae were the chief enemy. I did as many as 350 operations in one year for Entropion following trachoma. Ophthalmia neonatorum was another curse. A new-born babe got its infection from its mother. When its eyes got sore and it did not open them for several days, superstition would not allow her to leave home before the baby was two weeks old. Only after that did she set out for hospital. Alas, in most cases it was already too late; the child was blind for life due to the ulceration of its cornea. I saw this tragedy again and again. It is a condition which is entirely preventable if it is treated at once, and that is the function of modern asceptic midwifery. As our nurses

65

saw these cases they became clamorous for more training in midwifery. Other eye conditions treated were cataract, sympathetic ophthalmia, etc. This latter occurs in a good eye when an injured eye gets infected and neglected. To save the sight of the remaining good eye it is often necessary to remove entirely the injured eye. But how could this be done in this town where, not so many years before our own arrival, in Boxer days, printed accusations against all foreigners had been put out saying that the foreigners were 'gouging out children's eyes to make their medicines'? Nevertheless, as the years went on we were able to do even this service for the injured again and again! Of course it involved full explanations beforehand and a form-of-consent signed by the patient and his relatives before any operation. It meant much when we were so trusted by our patients.

Maternity

In our early years old custom and superstition together ensured that the only maternity cases that came to us were patients in the last stages of exhaustion and distress after some country 'Sarah Gamp' had done her worst. The case would be carried, perhaps for a two-day journey, on a stretcher by two men. Perhaps operation could save the mother. How grateful these families were when that was the case and she could go home safe and sound. But it needed years of work and propaganda before we could persuade any normal cases to trust us... Here again it was our Christian women who broke through the old taboos and led the way.

Our nurses were always on the alert for these cases, urging them to come in. One, Mo-fu-shih, would go out into the city streets and buttonhole any passing pregnant woman! Crude perhaps, but she wanted to help, and was quite likely to be effective.

Gradually numbers increased, until in 1943 we were able to open a new ward entirely for maternity cases. Business was then brisk. It reached its peak one day in 1949 when it was discovered that the surname of a new case was 'Mao'. She had come to us from the town of Siangtan, having chosen our hospital for her confinement. She was actually a niece of Mao Tse-Tung himself. She asked no special privileges, but our nurses were suddenly in the seventh heaven. After that, the reputation of our Maternity Department was safe for years to come!

A Grateful Patient

We always saw many cases of stone in the bladder at Shaoyang, sometimes over sixty of them in one year. We never really found out just why this was such a prevalent disease locally. Dietary errors have been suggested, or something in the water supply, or even excess sunshine while working in the fields.

One day a stranger appeared suffering from severe stone pain, but bringing no money for either food or medicine. He was admitted, operated on and sent home cured. Before he left someone must have told him the amount which he should have paid if he had not been on the free list. We heard no more from him—until eight years later I had a letter from a Presbyterian Mission Doctor at Hengyang enclosing a cheque for eight dollars. This sum had been handed to him to pass on to me by a man at his hospital Out-Patients Department, who told the story of having been operated on at Shaoyang long ago. He had been cured and he thought that perhaps one missionary had means of sending the money to another. It was our old stone patient, now quite well and earning his living as a pedlar taking cloth round to distant farms for sale. He had saved the money up during the years of his trading and now wanted to express his thanks for help given, and to repay his debt. Incidentally, he had also become a Christian in the meantime.

A Fractured Knee-cap

A coolie was carrying his heavy load from Shaoyang out into the country. Such a load, divided into two parts and carried at each end of his yoke or carry-pole, would weigh 150 pounds or more. He would expect to cover thirty miles a day. Twenty miles from town he tripped on some slight obstruction, something in his leg went snap and he could move no farther. He could but lie on one side of the path in severe pain. In those days and at that place there was no sort of ambulance or first aid service. A passing coolie consented to take over the burden, deliver it and take the pay. The injured man was just allowed to lie there as others passed by. Presently a Church member who was passing, stopped and spoke to him, telling him that he must somehow get to the Christian Hospital at Shaoyang, twenty miles away, but neither of them had money for transport. The man thereupon started to crawl to hospital on two hands and one leg! Such is life in a non-Christian land, where there is no Welfare State or sick-pay or the like. Two or three days later the man dropped exhausted at our hospital gate. Our gatekeeper saw him and brought him in. He was attended to at once. I diagnosed a fractured patella or knee-cap, which needed operation. He was washed, fed and put to bed, and in due time at operation the bone was wired into place. He made a perfect recovery and after some weeks was able to go home. I shall always remember his face as he said his thanks each time that I did a ward round. "I would not be alive if it were not for this hospital" were his words.

Here is a letter which came to me, in English, one day in 1943. The writer was one of many well-to-do refugees at that time coming inland away from the Japanese invasion. Even allowing for the customary flowery language, it is of interest as showing how some of those who crowded our Out-Patient Department saw it all.

National Teachers' College,
Lantien, Hunan,
June 3, 1943.

'Dear Doctor,
I have no doubt but that you are used to find your patients bear a profound sense of gratitude and admiration for the kind service you have been rendering them. But there is no reason why I should refrain from paying my homage to you when I am so inclined. I have been deeply impressed by you and your hospital, though I have only spent two mornings and have peeped here and there at the 'Pu-Ai' or 'Loving All Hospital'. A look at your cheerful countenance, a glimpse of the bevy of your kindly 'Nightingales', a glance over your grateful patients, these are enough even for a casual observer to have a fair idea of your work there.'

A paragraph follows about his brother who was then an eye patient in hospital. He ends: 'Believing that God will shower his blessings on the head of those who are living Evangelists to preach his Gospel of Love by actually doing a work of love for their fellow men,

I am, respectfully yours,
Liu Tien-nan.'

Hospital Orphans

Back to 1923—a famine year. Our first buildings were being erected. People were dying of hunger on the streets. We had empty beds in our new wards. We wanted to do something about it. We therefore went out into the city streets and picked out a dozen or so of the most pitiable boys sleeping on the streets (one proved to be a girl), and put them into empty beds. Before long, several of them were well enough to find their way home, but we were left with eight 'permanent patients', living entirely in hospital. We tried to make it their home. They went to the little school run by the Mission and learned to read and write. In due time, we apprenticed them one by one to local craftsmen, under the old Chinese system. One became our 'House Boy'. With most of them we soon lost touch and not all of them did well. I think that they never felt completely at home in the hospital. They still missed parents and clan and must have sensed deep down, some feeling of insecurity. Their hard experience and maladjustments resulted in several cases of petty thieving and the like. Of one or two of them I must say more.

A Riot

Little Liu was an orphan who came in during that famine of 1922-3. I first saw him when I was walking through the town, lying huddled up in the gutter (literally) outside the front door of a rich man's house. The rich man was also of the Liu clan. The boy was there perchance some scraps of food might be thrown on to the street by the servants. His body was sore and ulcerated and unimaginably dirty. He was perhaps, nine or ten years old. It seemed that there would be little hope of saving his life, but at least we could make his last few days comfortable. He was put to bed in the ward, washed and fed, but he remained huddled up. We could not get his legs straight. He also had a heavy infection with Ascaris worms. Rest and good food and simple medicine brought gradual improvement. First we were able to get him to lie straight in bed, next he managed to sit up, then to dangle his legs over the edge of the bed. Soon he was hobbling round the ward. Then his legs got stronger, though never perfect. Before long he too was able to go to school. He now told us that before the famine days he had been earning his own living as a coal coolie, carrying small loads of coal from pit-head to riverside, paid by the weight that he was able to deliver. As prices rose he could not earn enough for his own food, and when he had not enough to eat he carried less coal and was literally starving as well as ill, when we found him.

He did better at school than some of the others and presently passed on to a local higher primary run by the Government. In such a school he had to wear the regulation uniform. He still lived in hospital.

In December 1926 he would be about thirteen, but very small for his age. For December 25th the local revolutionaries had planned big demonstrations against the English and the Christians, urged on by the 'underground' as we now know. In North China there had been serious loss of life in such demonstrations. As the day approached

69

rumours were thick of trouble to come. We were advised to keep Christmas very quietly and make no outside decorations.

Christmas Day, 1926. I and the family and Sister Katie Castle were all in our bungalow, finishing a subdued Christmas dinner, when we saw a large crowd coming across the rice fields towards the hospital. As they came in view they shouted slogans in unison, 'Down with the English', etc., and came on. At once roughs pushed open the hospital front gate and the crowd of soldiers, roughs and school children poured into the compound. The pupils of all the government schools had been compelled to join the procession. Thus it was that little Liu found himself one of the crowd that day, wearing his school uniform. The crowd poured in and the roughs came in smashing up furniture or windows, bottles or pictures, and looting what they wanted. Noting the situation, most of the staff had made themselves scarce in good time and fled. Little Liu did not like what was going on. That day he had on his uniform and a special red braid as bugler. He also knew where the most valuable things in the hospital were kept, in the operating theatre. Quite on his own, he placed himself on sentry-go outside the operating room door. When rioters wanted to open that door he said: 'No. I am on duty. I am a Government student.' And away they went!

While all this was going on, I and the family in our bungalow were surrounded by a large section of the crowd. They were looking in at every window and trying every door, but were a bit sheepish when they saw us inside. We held a brief session of prayer and then it seemed right for me to try to get out into the garden by the back door. I got out, and when behind the crowd, called to them that it was time to go home, as I was going to shut the main gate. I heard them mutter 'He doesn't know what's on'. Arriving in the hospital at the lower end of the compound I met chaos. By that time several soldiers who had been patients in bed, had got up and formed some rope into long whips, which they were lashing in all directions trying to move the crowd. With this encouragement the crowd soon began to melt away. The staff dared to come out of hiding and order was gradually restored.

While I was busy thus Mary in the bungalow had had difficulty with one man in the crowd surrounding our house. He had put his foot through a window in the dining room. She saw who had done it and immediately asked him why he had done it and then invited him to come in if he really wanted to see what the house was like. He came in alone! He was shown round each room and then politely

70

bowed out. None lifted a finger to hurt or injure, and the crowd was soon all gone.

When we had time to look round that Christmas evening the whole of the Out-Patients' Department was a shambles. But the operating room was untouched. Little orphan Liu, by himself, had saved all that. No one had told him to do anything. He had seen an opportunity and with a magnificent bluff had done what no one else could do that day for His Hospital.

Liu continued to live with us for some years after that. He eventually became a singer of old style opera music with a travelling company and used to come in and see his old friends from time to time.

Another of the boys trained as a tailor, and did good work for many years as an independent workman, many of his customers being found from staff and patients.

Telling the Good News

As soon as I had learned enough Chinese to talk fairly freely, when our first buildings came into use I began a habit which continued, of going down to the wards on a Sunday afternoon with my violin. I would sit on the edge of a patient's bed (scandalizing the nurses) and play a tune or teach the verse of a hymn. Then I would tell in the simplest words one of the great Gospel stories ... the Prodigal Son, the Lost Sheep, or those first verses of John's Gospel, which though so profound, use such very plain and simple words or phrases. (This holds just as much in Russian or in Chinese as in English.) How they listened, those simple peasant folk, nearly all of them people who had never heard a word of it all before. What a privilege it was to be able to talk to them thus. Yes—and we often had an underground Communist with us as a patient, listening too. They knew what we were doing all those years. They told me so after they came to power.

Of course, most working days allowed me no off-time for this sort of activity. We always worked in close touch with our evangelistic workers, who came and went as they saw fit. Usually we also had a local church member of some standing and ability, who was called out by the church as a sort of liaison man amidst our crowds of patients. His job was to make friends with the patients, explaining some of the ways of this strange, foreign hospital to them, and always ready to sell to them a small copy of one of the gospels. He was our 'hospital evangelist'.

The Bathing Pond Incident

Twenty yards away, outside our front gate, was an old mud pond. A stone-lined well close by it evidently marks the site of an ancient water source from which we drew for our daily needs. In hot weather many small boys enjoyed a splash in the pond and the women did their washing there. One day, it was 1930, I noticed a crowd standing by the pond, talking and gesticulating. Next I saw Mr Dang Pang-mei our male assistant running towards me. A boy had been bathing in the pond and could not be found. No one dare to go into that water to get him out because of their fear of the devils. Would I join him and go into the water and try and find the boy? That was a very unexpected challenge. Dang was a Christian. Off we went together into the crowd, and throwing off our outer garments only, we jumped in. There was no sign at all of the boy. The water was thick with opaque red mud, and the pond about seven feet deep. By treading water with my feet down I was eventually able to feel something below me in the deepest part. It then did not take long to get him ashore, though he was quite dead.

I have always been glad that Dang Pang-mei acted as he did that day. It was a piece of powerful Christian witness, with never a word spoken. It spoke where the old superstitions are most binding. A Christian need no longer fear the old devils. Also folk were very grateful for help given.

Gate-keeper Lei

About 1930, an old soldier, Lei Ch'in-kwang, having left the army had found a cushy job as a local, old regime, tax collector. He had to pay so much a year for the job. He then had to sit in a roadside shop and collect a small tax from every coolie bringing goods into town from the country. These takings were all his own and he could hope for a good profit on the transaction for he could easily over-charge any uneducated coolies.

He had his office next door to our hospital main gate, and when business was slack he would wander into hospital and listen to Evangelist Tsao, or buy a Gospel. Reading brought conviction, especially when he read of Levi sitting 'at the receipt of custom', the very same job as his own! He concluded he could no longer remain in a dishonest job. He threw up his work and retired to his clan home in the countryside, and tried to earn a living by buying loads of country rice, carrying it to town and selling for a slightly increased price.

All through this period I knew nothing about him. Not long after, the job of Hospital Gatekeeper fell vacant. Our gatekeeper, Mr Tsao, was also the Out-Patient Registration clerk and he ventured to bring forward Lei's name as a possible candidate. He was appointed and from then on we found that we had a real colleague at the gate house.

At the gate he was always the first man whom strangers coming to hospital had to contact. He would talk to them in their own broad colloquial, dissipate their fears and tell them what to do if they needed to see the doctor. He was invaluable in many ways. If there was a riot outside he knew just when to shut the gates and when to re-open. He never complained about night calls. He knew when un-authorized strollers were trying to get past on false pretences. An old soldier was just the man for the job. In and out of revolutions and wars he just carried on and came up smiling. Here indeed was a loyal servant of his Master Jesus, a true and faithful Christian!

An early incident in the hospital work is retold by Rev. E. G. Kampenhausen who, in February 1929 was a young German missionary on the staff of the Liebenzeller branch of the C.I.M. in Shaoyang. He was living at their compound inside the city, a mile or more from our hospital, which is outside the city proper.

Very late one evening his wife came into labour with their first child. He at once rushed to the hospital to get medical help. Without delay he and I started out on foot for his home, but by then the great East Gate of the city had been closed and barred for the night. 'Kai Men', 'Open the gate', we cried, but the soldier on guard inside took no notice of our cry nor of any explanation. We were shut out. What could we do?

Mr Kamphausen continues: 'But you did not give up. You walked with me through the dark narrow outer streets, round the foot of the city wall to the Peh Men, the North Gate, facing the river. You pushed against that big gate, and it opened a bit. At once the armed guard called and threatened, you told him of the emergency and he reluctantly "did not hinder" us.

'Inside the city the curfew was on. All the streets were empty of people except for the guard, rifle at the ready, at every street corner. After being challenged three more times we at last reached the mission station . . . and you stayed with us that night. How can I forget your love and ministry to us as a family. And we were *not* British.'

CHAPTER EIGHT

Outside Four Walls

DURING my years at Shaoyang it was only very occasionally that I got an opportunity of leaving the daily routine of the hospital and getting out into the deep countryside on a country tour like my minister colleagues. One of these infrequent opportunities occurred in 1942, when the presence of an extra doctor on duty in the hospital set me free. Normally I felt that I could be of more use to my patients if I stayed in hospital, ready with staff and equipment to give effective treatment to the many who came, rather than wandering round the country handing out a few tablets to a clamouring crowd who hardly knew how to use them. The best result from a village visit was when it gave some few people courage to come themselves to hospital for operation or other needed treatment.

When 'on tour' one would walk ten or fifteen miles to some small village centre and hold a service or two. In my case, the rest of the day was then occupied dealing with an unending succession of people with every complaint or none, until night came and we all turned in for a few hours' rest, then next day on to another village.

A visit to Pai-Tsang-Ssu, nearly fifty miles south in Shaoyang area was typical. Here the resident preacher was old Mr Mao, sixty-five—very old for a Chinese villager—and half blind, but he was a force to be reckoned with, for two of his village boys have since been ordained to the ministry. A trip of twenty miles was through gorgeous limestone scenery of green hills and rich rice lands. His 'church' is just a rented, wooden shop on the dark and narrow village street. He was expecting me and had put up a bed in a dark little cubby hole at the back of the shop for my convenience. I had hardly arrived when a deputation consisting of the village head-man, his deputy, two school masters and the village constable arrived to offer an official welcome. Family prayers that evening developed into a free-for-all meeting, open to all the village. My fiddle came in useful.

The next day, Sunday, was a full one. Up at dawn, I got a brief quiet time out in the woods behind the village with a woodpecker at work. At breakfast the crowds were already gathering. After a short talk to them I had to begin to treat the sick. I sat in the shop front, fenced round by one or two benches and with my stock-in-trade in front of me on a small table, like a pedlar at a fair. Patients came non-stop till I was called to lunch with Mr Mao. At 2 p.m. he and I went out to make a few calls in the village and then on again interviewing patients until dusk, when Mao again came along and appealed to me to stop, as it was time for the evening service. Then supper and to bed in my little dark hole, with small boys looking through the chinks between the boards to satisfy their curiosity. The end of a perfect day. Similar steps at other villages, with variations, and so after ten days back again to hospital.

At another time I had a somewhat similar trip in North Hunan together with C. G. Baker. We travelled this time through country only recently laid waste by Communist guerrilla forces. Villages had been depopulated and the Red Forces still in the hills were only twenty miles away. I found the cause at Tai-Chia-Ping (Tai Family Village) of special interest. This is the family home of Mr Tai Chang-ching, formerly preacher at Shaoyang, but now aged 73 and living in retirement. He still finds much to do. He still preaches to his own people and has five or six little country congregations within easy reach, all meeting in farmhouse rooms set aside for worship. His people are all farmers, of the earth earthy.

Mr Tai told me how he got new members: 'They all come to me,' he said, 'and ask me to pray for them when they are ill, but I refuse unless they will first promise to leave their idols: throw them away, in fact. They then come to worship the true God, and I pray. And they do come.' He had quite a group of his people asking for baptism by Mr Baker. This is a station where religion works. Mr Tai is a trusted leader of his own people. Surely here prayer for the sick is being used in the true gospel manner.

Highway Robbery

It was when we got out into the open country, outside four walls, that unexpected things began to happen.

As Christain missionaries we never carried firearms, and during most of these years brigandage was rife. We were usually given plenty of advice beforehand if any road was considered 'unsafe', and we did not go looking for trouble. When travel was necessary in the course of our work, well that was that, and we went ahead and felt quite safe. Were we not on our Master's business? The following incidents are mostly from our early days, long before the internal combustion engine reached Shaoyang. The sedan chair, carried on the shoulders of two coolies, was our vehicle—or Shanks's Pony.

On one occasion I was bringing my small family back to Shaoyang. We had covered most of the 150 miles from Changsha and were lodged for the night at the village of Chu-Tan-Pu, thirty miles from home. Cook Lo was travelling with us. We had all just got to bed after the long day's march when I heard Lo knocking at our door. Would I please open the door as the customs man wanted to see us? Certainly a queer request at that time and place. I got up, opened the door, and there was the most typical stage bandit I ever saw! He was armed and wore a very ragged soldier's uniform. Behind him was Lo, now gesticulating violently to warn me to be careful. I tumbled to what was doing. No words were needed as the man had his rifle at his hip ready to shoot. I greeted him politely and asked what he wanted. 'Money', was his gruff reply. I tried to bargain. It was near the end of our journey and I knew there were only six dollars left in our baggage. I produced three and gave them to him, but he wanted much more. At this point Mary, still half asleep, called out to me: 'Tell him to be quiet or he'll wake the baby.' I replied, in an aside: 'Be quiet. He's a bandit.' She said no more. Suddenly a bugle sounded outside, and the bandit turned and left us without another word, taking his three dollars with him. He had evidently been called off by his chief. Later that same night we heard shots being fired in the village, but we were not molested further.

We were glad to get home the next day. Such bandits are often just neglected and out-of-work soldiers trying to make a living.

A Night near Siang-Siang

A few years later I was returning alone along that same road after some meetings in Changsha. It was winter and I was wearing a long sheepskin coat with a fancy rabbit-fur collar, perhaps rather plutocratic. The second night out I put up at a small inn near Siang-Siang. I had gone to bed in the one big room together with several of my coolies, but half way through the night was awaked by a big explosion just outside the unglazed window of my room. This was soon followed by a splintering of wood as the front doors of the inn were broken open and several men armed dashed into our room. One of them kept me covered with his gun and no one was allowed to speak. The others proceeded to force open all my baggage, taking what they fancied, including the big overcoat. But they missed my watch. Having satisfied themselves they left us to finish the night.

We were on the road again at dawn, a bright and frosty morning and I did miss that coat! When I reached Yungfeng, the German missionary there, Mr Schindewolf, insisted that I borrow his overcoat but as he is a small man, it was not a good fit. After getting home I did report this robbery to the civilian authorities, but my letter was never even acknowledged. Rumour later said that they had recovered the coat and taken some action. I never saw the coat again.

Shooting the Rapids

Occasionally we travelled to Changsha down the river Tzu instead of the overland route. This meant shooting the many rapids, in a river junk, a small house-boat, twenty to thirty feet long, covered amid-ships by a solid bamboo tent. Such travel can be very comfortable. There is a mast and sail, and two very large side-oars, each manned by two or three men. An even larger third oar projects from the bows and needs several men to work it. It gives immense steering power when in the rapids amidst rocks and whirlpools.

On one such journey I had with me a preacher, Mr Tseng, and his family, also several schoolgirls going to Yiyang school. No boatman ever starts down these dangerous rapids without first sacrificing a chicken and scattering its blood and feathers on the prow of the boat. The blood is shed to propitiate the spirits of the river so that they may have a safe voyage. When we were passengers they did this before we came aboard, but the blood and feathers were plain to see.

Sailing downstream we got off to a good start. About noon someone on the bank shouted a message to our taipan (captain), and at once all was consternation. The message was that just round the next bend of the river, at the big rapids, a band of robbers was holding up all ships for ransom and shooting indiscriminately. We pulled into the bank. Could we, dare we, go on? I suggested a short prayer meeting. Then and there we asked for guidance. It soon seemed right for myself and our servant boy to go ashore and to walk downstream to where the trouble was. We could not sail upstream against the current. If you meet a man face to face you can talk to him, but you can't talk to anybody from a boat under fire in the rapids. I carried nothing but my paper umbrella. I and the boy had not gone far before we sighted a man on sentry-go beside the path in front of us. He was armed with a big knife tied to the end of a long broomstick. As we approached he did not challenge us, but fell in in front of us, and so we approached the little wooden riverside village of Ch'in-Ch'i-Tan. The village appeared to be very full of men in soldier's uniforms, resting and gambling at the inn tables.

They looked rather surprised to see us. I sat down on a vacant bench and asked to see their 'officer', giving my printed visiting card to one of the men to deliver to him. Taking the card he disappeared inside. Meanwhile I talked with the men, treating them as if they were regular soldiers. One of them came forward and claimed to be a recent patient of mine at Shaoyang. He still had a lump in his neck. 'Could I cure it?' Examining it I found a badly swollen gland. I

77

could offer no treatment on the spot. If he would go back to hospital I would arrange the needed operation. 'Can't you do the operation for me here and now?' 'Alas, no,' I said, 'I have no instruments, no knife here. It can't be done.' 'Won't this knife do?' he replied, pulling a dagger from his belt and handing it to me. 'No, that is the wrong kind of knife.' I replied.

Our chat was interrupted by the entry of a young military officer in uniform, their 'chief'. He was worried. Had I soldiers with me? Or arms? What did I want? I told him that all I wanted was an unhindered passage for my boat, now waiting upstream. The men, now friendly, joined in the conversation. He eventually agreed to send my boy back with one of his own men to tell the boat to come on, while I should walk on down stream to board the boat below the rapids. It was indeed in fear and trembling that that boatload came along, but the robbers were as good as their word and I was soon on board again.

It was some years later that Mary and Mrs Stanfield, travelling down that same river with the children, had quite a hair-raising time when their boatman had an altercation with a Customs official and pushed the said official into the water. The fat was then in the fire, and the officials wanted to impound the boat and all its passengers. In the end all was settled in a true Chinese manner and the journey continued happily. The guilty boatman rejoined them a few miles downstream.

A Great Wind

Oh how often we have felt so wonderfully protected, Mary and I! In times of storm or stress of many different sorts. I recall one time when we were staying on our very isolated summer mountain, twenty miles from Shaoyang, called Tung-Kwang-Ai (Copper Ore Peak). Local politics were unsettled. A roving Red Army was said to be approaching Changsha. Word came through from our Chairman to say we ought to come downhill at once and try to join him in Changsha before the invaders could arrive, and go down river with him. We started to pack at once for an early start next morning. Overnight a huge wind-storm arose. Wind and rain were such that next morning it was quite impossible to get coolies and children down those narrow, steep and slippery paths. We had perforce to wait overnight. But the next day it was worse, and for three solid days we could not move.

At last, when the rain did stop, the only route possible was to go down the far side of the mountain to Ch'in-Ch'i-Tan, where the

River Tzu cuts its way through a steep gorge—the same place where I met that robber band on the occasion just described. Friendly Chinese soon found us a boat going down the river to Yiyang, not to Changsha. When we reached Hankow and Kuling after many days of travel we found that if we had gone down as first instructed we should have been running right into Communist war and disorder. . . but did not God send that mighty wind to direct us?

Evacuation from Shaoyang, 1927.

Just before Christmas, 1926, the big oil store at Shaoyang, owned by Socony of New York was set on fire by student agitators. There had been similar riots all over the country, and a nation-wide campaign against British and Americans, jointly defined as 'Imperialists'. Our Chinese friends were full of forebodings. Our Chairman had warned us that we might have to leave if things got worse. As Medicals we thought that we could stay on, even when some of our colleagues did leave. Then followed the doings of Christmas Day 1926, which I have described in the story of little Liu.

Soon after the New Year, definite orders came to us from our Chairman to evacuate at once. We were then Mary and myself, Andrew, aged four, and Eleanor, six, and Baby Philip, eight months, and Sister Katie Castle. Obediently we got packed and started the chair journey towards Changsha. Although all towns were very disturbed, we met no trouble in the villages we passed. Half-way to Changsha we called at Siang-Siang to see our German C.I.M. friends, Mr and Mrs Seeliger. Here we found a letter awaiting us from Mr Pillow (Acting Chairman) informing us of the death from illness of the Chairman, G. G. Warren. He warned us not to try to enter Changsha, where the agitation was at its height, but to try to make our way by river all the way to Hankow. This would be a much less conspicuous mode of travel.

We could get a small boat from Siang-Siang. The Seeligers were generosity itself, supplying us with food and all things needful for a long trip down river. Being German, he could move freely in town. He found a boat for us and got it anchored outside city limits. At dusk we all embarked quietly and un-noticed. (I still remember some lovely Kohlrabi which Mr Seeliger brought along from his own garden, and a small cooking stove that was very useful.)

Slipping downstream we soon reached the main river Siang near Siangtan. Here to our amazement we found a bridge of boats across the river, holding up all traffic, and huge crowds crossing it to join in the burning of the British oil installation, already well

79

alight. We could only wait. Our cook, Lo-ssu-fu, took the precaution of fixing up a cloth screen to prevent outsiders seeing the white faces in our boat. And so we waited, and slept, overnight. Next morning the bridge had gone and we continued north to Changsha.

Just short of the town of Changsha we pulled inshore and Lo-ssu-fu went alone to try to contact Mr Pillow. He soon returned with the news. Feelings in town were still running high. Mr Warren's funeral was being held that morning in the Christian cemetery south of the city, not far from where our boat then was. Pillow suggested that I go to the funeral and we could meet there. I knew the lie of the land so I at once skipped off, over rice-fields and hills, until I saw the funeral party in the distance. I was thus able to take part in our farewells to a long-loved and trusted leader. A short talk with Pillow and I got my orders that we should go as straight as possible for home, our furlough being due. And so we parted there in that cemetery, he to return to his difficult assignment, I back to my anxious family in the boat.

The further journey needed a larger boat, but a transfer was easily made and at dawn next day we were off again. Progress was slow against a head wind and we failed to find any steam launch to give us a tow. Very early on the second morning, before daylight, Baby Philip began crying for something. This woke the boatman— we were all sleeping under the one tent roof. He looked out, saw that the wind had dropped, and together his mate and he started to row. As daylight dawned I noticed a small foreign-type motor launch tied to the bank and just starting up his engines. We hailed him and the Chinese captain brought his launch alongside us, told us to hitch on alongside, and off we went at a great pace across the dreary wastes of the shallow Tungting Lake. In double-quick time we were at the little lake port of Tseng-ling-chi, near Yo Hsien, and he pulled us in among a lot of junks similar to our own. We wondered, what next?

Dare we show ourselves? Suddenly, as we looked out through the chinks of our boat-tent Mary saw a foreigner in a boat quite close to us. It was Mr Stanfield, who was evacuating from Pingkiang, like ourselves! We were all soon out of our hiding and busy talking twenty to the dozen. Soon other colleagues emerged, six junk loads of us in all. Some had been ten days crossing that lake which we had covered in a few hours.

Our helpful launch captain now agreed to take all six boats on tow to Hankow. He got us roped together in two groups of three, himself in front to tow the lot. Again he started off at a great pace.

C. Mary Pearson, a photograph taken in China, about 1947

George H. Pearson, 1967 (Photo: Allison Studio, Armagh)

Doctors and nurses at Shaoyang, 1932

Staff and students at Shaoyang Methodist Hospital, 1946—the group who
got the hospital working after the Japanese evacuation. The photograph
was taken after a welcome to Dr Andrew Pearson, just arrived in China

As we got nearer Hankow the north wind rose again and the river really got rough. Our wooden junks rocked and crushed against each other as the tow ropes strained. I felt that the junks could hardly stand it and had my penknife ready to cut us loose if it got worse. But we did come through into calmer water. The launch drew us up against the deserted bund at Hankow and then at once went off, without even a goodbye, and without asking a penny for his services which had been so valuable!

At Hankow. The British Navy takes a Hand

Hankow is usually a very busy centre, people everywhere, but as we arrived all was silent and deserted. What had we run into? Had all English folk already left? Rumour told us of an important political agreement signed a day or two earlier between the British Consul and China. What was happening? Now we had to try to find out. We discussed it together and it was decided that Stanfield and myself, as the two senior men, should go at once ashore and try to contact the Consul, if any, and get instructions. We found the Consul on duty as usual, were kindly received and told to stay where we were overnight. In due time he would arrange our passage down river. No trouble, no danger. We returned at once to our families with the good news to find all in utter confusion. It seemed that after we had left for the Consul's, a junior colleague had had the bright idea of trying to find the British admiral on a sloop in the river. He found his admiral and returned to our boats with a fully armed landing party of British Marines, under the command of a Lieutenant Stevenson, a friend of Royalty! They had been sent to rescue a lost party of English women and children from all the terrible dangers of China! In fact, such an armed party was in far greater danger than ourselves, for by landing they were invading Chinese territory.

When we tried to explain the instructions we had from the Consul, our families wanted to stay where they were, but the Lieutenant would listen to nothing. We did not want to go but he threatened to arrest any of us who would not go with him. Only under that threat did we move. Little did he realize what he was talking about when he generously said that his men would bring all the luggage along. The children's bedding was all laid out for use on the floor of the boat. Pots, pans, bedding, furniture, etc., all loose, and in use for the past two weeks, all boxes opened and unpacked, everything every-where. We just had to make the best of it and let them move things anyhow. Fortunately the town was still asleep so there was no trouble for the armed invaders. We were soon on a comfortable

British steamer but the man who fetched the Admiral had to stay behind in town to see about the removal of his piano! Otherwise we eventually found all our things, all, that is, except Stanfield's typewriter. He lost that. Eighteen months later, when he was able to return to Hunan and to his station at Pingkiang, it was returned to him by the boatman. When he (the boatman) had seen all the rumpus in Hankow he had feared that he would not be paid, so secreted the typewriter as payment on account. But as all the boatmen were paid in full he was glad to return it to its owner at the first opportunity. We always found these simple boatmen scrupulously honest.

Travelling down the Yangtse next day, we passed Kiukiang, the port for Kuling where Christine, aged six, had been left at school. We made enquiries but were told that the school and children had already been evacuated to Shanghai. Arrived in Shanghai we found ourselves 'interesting refugees from the interior'. A whole bevy of English ladies from the British Women's Association boarded our boat to see what they could do for us. We asked one of them if she could help us find Christine. 'Oh yes,' was her reply, 'she has come here and is staying with a Mr Pugh.' Did that warm my Mary's heart! And so we were re-united. It was all quite wonderful. They also found us temporary accommodation, and a week or two later we were on board the Japanese liner, *Hakozaki Maru*, headed for London. God does lead us in unusual ways.

Hot Weather. Mountain Holidays at Tung-Kwang-Ai

Yes, we did get a holiday sometimes, when the weather got rather too hot for work in the summer. Winter in Hunan was always mild, with an occasional frost or a rare fall of snow. Summers were almost tropical, with a very high humidity and plenty of mosquitoes; not all of them malaria carriers, but none-the-less uncomfortable.

When we arrived it was already an established custom, and especially for the mothers with children, to go up to the Lushan mountains in Kiangsi where Kuling was already a busy summer resort, 3,500 feet above sea-level. But we soon found that travel from Shaoyang to Kuling took us ten days each way by chair, boat, etc. I therefore joined up with one of the German C.I.M. workers, Mr Schoppe, to investigate the possibility of using some nearer height. He had contacts twenty miles from Shaoyang amongst some beautiful hills. At the foot of the hills was a large, old Buddhist Monastery and a smaller temple nearer the top, 3,300 feet up, with an old nun in charge. This was Tung-Kwang-Ai. The nun had relatives who had become Christians. She therefore welcomed us and offered us the use of two rooms in her temple. These rooms were built of wood only. Cows occupied the ground floor. We could look between the floorboards to watch the cows below. Flies were the chief nuisance, but our mosquito nets kept them at bay during nights. The coolness, after the hot plains, was very acceptable. Schoppe had put up a small bungalow nearby.

The country in the hills around was always very unsettled, but our nun seemed to know all the local bad characters, who held her in awe. She was known as Tu-Fei-Niang, 'Robbers' Mother'. We never experienced the slightest trouble when staying in those lovely, steep, green valleys, far away from all normal government or police supervision.

In the following years I was able to buy a small site nearby for a bungalow, and using local materials, to complete a four-bedroom house plus kitchen, etc., for only £100 in English money! We had many happy times there, but it was always lonely and some years we let others use our bungalow while we made the long trip to Kuling to meet colleagues and see something of the big world outside.

Surgery in the Farmyard

One night after we had retired, we were aroused by many distant shouts, and noises. A string of lights appeared coming round the mountainside. We could only wonder what was afoot in this lonely place. Were the local robbers at last coming for us in force? Our servants were as troubled as ourselves. We waited trembling, as knocks came at our outside gate.

It proved to be a group of about twenty men with torches, carrying with them a woman who had just cut her own throat. She was still alive and they had heard that there was a doctor on the mountain. They dumped her in the yard used by our cow, and it was up to me. I retreated into the house, borrowed my wife's needles and cotton, got them boiled, found a bottle of Lysol and some warm water. There in the farmyard, by the light of their torches and a hurricane lamp, I cleaned the wound and sewed her up. We were able to find a corner for her and her escort in a small room beside the kitchen. How grateful they all were as the torchbearers prepared to return the way they had come. Next day we got the woman carried the twenty miles to hospital where she could have proper care. She was there several weeks, eventually making quite a fair recovery.

Another time when I was approaching Tung-Kwang-Ai I was stopped in some fields by a man with bad toothache. Could I help?

My only available tool was a penknife, but using a bit of leverage, the tooth came out as we stood there in the rice fields, to his great satisfaction.

'Nan-Yoh' or 'Hengshan' is a Hunan mountain which we visited sometimes in our later years as it is much nearer Changsha and easier to reach for many people. It is one of the five historic sacred peaks of China, and it is crowded with temples and monasteries. Before the days of revolution it was visited yearly by hundreds of thousands of pilgrims each year. G. G. Warren made a number of visits to it, being greatly thrilled at the opportunity which he found of preaching to these pilgrims, but in these new days there is but a handful of pilgrims treading the old roads. C. V. Cook and his two boys were at Nan Yoh one summer and they often used to play in a small stream near the house. One day when they were called in to dinner, they said as they came in: 'Mummy, we've seen the tiger! He just stayed in the bushes by the stream and looked at us.' Mother was disinclined to believe, but questioning failed to shake their story. 'He had big round eyes and a big round face.' Well, after all, tigers are known on those mountains!

The God of the Mountain

One time, about 1941, I was travelling alone along some of the rice field paths near the foot of the Nan Yoh mountains. I and my coolie arrived at a wayside inn and sat down for a meal. As we waited for our rice, an old man appeared and set up some incense sticks to burn in a bowl at the front door of the inn. The door itself opened on to the road and a glorious view of the Nan Yoh mountain, the Sacred Southern Peak, whose top was that day snow-covered due to the winter cold.

Slowly the old man knelt down and kow-towed, knocking his head on the pavement several times—and as he prayed thus towards the sacred mountain he spoke aloud to the God of the Mountains, whose name is Sheng-ti, the Holy God; and I marvelled as I heard the words of this heathen man's prayer. 'Oh God, help me,' he prayed. 'This man loves you, won't you love this man in return. Won't you help him?' The words that he used were just those that we so often use in Christian worship. What aspiration! What a need!

'Sheng Ti' is the old Animistic local deity of this mountain. He is worshipped every year by the thousands of pilgrims who flock to the mountain shrines. Even his name is so like the name the Chinese Churches use for God, 'Shang Ti', the 'God-above-all.' Only the slight difference of the vowel sound.

Was this an opportunity for witness? Alas, I was tired and intent on completing my long day's thirty-mile walk, and I missed saying anything to that man. But perhaps I, myself, learned something.

I Meet a Hermit

I was again at Nan Yoh in 1948. A small party of us had walked up to the summit and were returning along the narrow mountain path. I was last in the file and it had begun to rain. Rather than get wet I halted for shelter at a little stone temple beside the path, not far from the summit. In the temple was a gaily dressed monk or hermit, dressed in a patchwork coat of many colours and sitting Buddha-like on a small carved stone table. He had a good roof over him but open all round, rather like a bandstand. He was quietly reading his Buddhist sutras aloud to himself. As I waited, standing beside him, he stopped and spoke to me and we talked. He told me that he used to be a high-ranking officer in Chiang Kai-shek's army. Tiring of the futilities of military life he left it, and now lives alone in this little old mountain temple. He lives very simply on casual gifts or on roots and grasses which he finds on the mountainside. He showed me how he lives. He never lies down at night, but rests sitting up in a sort of cupboard so small that he cannot lie down. It was eighteen years since he gave up his army life and he was now 74 years old. He did not tell me his name, probably he left that behind him too.

Sitting on his stone table on that mountain path, he looked just like a living Buddha. What a life! All by himself every day for all those years. Yet I felt that there was something sincere and satisfied about him. He had no wish to return to his old life in the world.

Yes, there is something very special about this sacred mountain of Nan Yoh. It has an atmosphere which I found nowhere else in China.

CHAPTER NINE

Staffing the Hospital

Nursing—Nurse Training

As WORK increased I soon found a need for help in all the many duties of the hospital, but especially for nurses. One trained boy and an assistant could not do everything. Girls in Hunan had never had nursing experience. In those days girls from a decent family would not be allowed out for such 'dirty work' and especially they would not be allowed to help any *man* from another family. When our first nurse from England, Sister Katie Castle, came therefore, we tried the old scheme of training a few young boys. But this never worked well. When they had been in hospital for a few months they usually felt that they knew everything and left suddenly to set up their own surgery in a shop in town. This was satisfactory neither to them nor to us.

Not until 1928, by which time Sister Maud Millican had succeeded Miss Castle, were we able to make the big step forward and attempt the training of girl nurses. Local mission schools were asked to suggest suitable candidates. We began with four girls, all from Christian homes, whose families were willing for them to come. They broke the taboo. Their names were Tsao Chu-hsioh, Wu Lu-teh (Ruth), Fang Li and Chen Peng. All of them did well. Sister Maud was just the right person to help them through their first difficult days. She was down with them first thing in the morning showing them just how to care for their patients. When they saw that even she did what they had always considered servant's work, such as giving or emptying bed-pans, or washing the dirtiest of patients on admission, they began to grasp something of what loving Christian service could mean. Before long she had them, not only working in the women's ward, but in the men's ward also and in this, we were, I believe, the very first hospital to do this in Hunan, and even in all Central China: though some of the hospitals had trained girls in women's wards only for many years.

From the first we kept the standards high, and it was soon arranged for them to take the full course of the newly formed Nurses' Association of China with their carefully supervised system of examinations. We were able to insist on a proper Middle School Certificate before starting and each entrant had to provide a guarantor, and to pay something towards the cost of her first year's training. After some years, at the urgent request of the girls, we switched over to take the newly offered Chinese Government Certificate, but our experience

86

of this was that it was merely a literary test of writing and of civics and general knowledge, with little or no attempt to test their knowledge of practical ward work. They had to give much time to the study of subjects such as 'The necessity of resisting the United Nations' or, 'Why the Chinese Republic is so much stronger than the Imperialist Countries'. Perhaps this was a product of the unsettled years and no doubt the later Communist regime would see to it that real work was given its rightful place in their training.

But Miss Millican was transferred to Yungchow. We then had Sister Freda Wright (later Mrs Willoughby of Yungchow Hospital). She was followed by China-born Dorothy Dymond, who had the great misfortune of trying to pass through Hong Kong on the day it was taken by the Japanese, and was held in a concentration camp for four years. Hilda Hudson came out to supply the vacancy in 1946. Her coal-black hair, as dark as any of her Chinese pupils, was a great asset to her. But she soon married Doctor Graham Watt of the C.M.S.

Sister Gertrude Hughes, from Rhyl in North Wales, was the last of our line of British Matrons. She joined us rather unexpectedly in 1948 only a few months before the Communist invasion and capture of our city. Before we finally left Shaoyang she was able to hand over full control to one of our senior graduates, Miss Hu Pei-Chi, C.R.N., a local Christian girl, who was elected to the job by a unanimous vote of students and staff.

But of Gertrude, I must say something more. Although she was with us barely three years, her time included the months of runaway inflation and disorder, and then all of the Communist take-over with their constant interference in every aspect of life.

I remember how, soon after the Reds had got to work, she came to me one day almost in tears, because the nurses had refused to obey an order she had given them, which conflicted with a Party order to attend some meeting or other. I had to explain that we were now living in the days of social revolution, and it might be that she would have to give way and allow the new ways of doing things, and rather to work with and through them. She took me at my word, and from then on she worked 'with' the nurses, rather than 'over' them. She was one of them but was always able to see that the patients got what they needed, and that they were cared for by happy nurses.

I saw how, when the nurses had to go to one of the many compulsory political meetings, they would come up to her and say: 'Please, Miss Hughes, will you come on duty now, we have to go out? She at once put on her uniform and took over the care of the ward herself until they returned. As soon as they were back they would come to her again. 'Please, Miss Hughes, you may go off duty now, we will look after everything,' and back the Matron went to her off-duty time. I shudder to think of what some English Matrons might have said—but not Gertrude. So well was she in with her girls, that during that last summer they even got her to join their open-air bathing parties in the river, half a mile away. She was one of them.

Boys and Girls

Another difficulty in those days was the problem of boy and girl relationships. One day during the 'Produce, produce' campaign, I heard a cheerful noise outside my window. Looking out I saw a boy nurse with a Chinese spade or machete on the soil bank at the side of the tennis lawn preparing to grow cabbages, and various girls noisily encouraging him. The previous day I had met several girls hanging on to a boy student, trying to recover some book he had taken. This was quite a new freedom between Chinese young people, and even the rough play is part of the new order. It is certainly better than the old method of giving a bad mark in Matron's copy book.

I have often felt that our work of nurse training was the best and most lasting part of the work done at Shaoyang. One saw the new arrivals as they came in to join a class, silly, giggling little schoolgirls, much like schoolgirls anywhere at say sixteen or younger, irresponsible and not knowing what to do next. But after graduation and perhaps six months on the staff as Sister, they were different people. Upstanding, responsible women, knowing what to do and how to do it. There was always a waiting list of jobs asking for our trained girls for Government and other hospitals.

It was in bringing all the work of past years to such a satisfying fruition during the days of Revolution that Gertrude Hughes's name must always be honoured.

I have no complete list of all our graduates. Wu lu-teh, a brilliant student, was last heard of married, and in charge of the deserted British Red Cross Station at Shanghai. Chen Peng became a physical instructor. Tsao Chu-hsioh after years of loyal service moved to the big hospital in Changsha, where her methods of personal service, learned at Shaoyang, were almost an embarrassment to her amongst nurses of a different tradition. An Hwa-shih, daughter of a Lutheran pastor married, and I met her many years later doing wonderful work in a clinic for refugees in Hong Kong, a true

88

missionary to her own people. And there was Hao Chih-Mei of whom more later.

During the early days of the Communist Liberation, the school went through new adventures, some of them described elsewhere. Immediately after the occupation many of the younger girls were attracted away by the thrill of all the new propaganda. Others, while sympathetic to the undoubted good parts of Communism, remained at their work, being told that that was the best way in which they could serve the new society. In those days it became increasingly difficult for any girl to take an open stand as a Christian. If she did, she was a marked person.

But during our last weeks in Shaoyang we saw the formation of what I like to call a small hard core of Christian girls in the school. At least three of the junior girls became much more regular at church and even at things like saying their prayers in the dormitory, full of scoffing schoolmates. Seeing this, we could not but give thanks. It was then that we ourselves were 'eased out' and had to return to England, and we could neither see nor hear more.

In the spring of 1949 I had a severe attack of flu, and while thus out of condition, I severely sprained my back by suddenly lifting a bundle of six hundred heavy silver dollars needed in hospital. For the next four days I could not stand up at all and had to stay in bed. Mary was away, but our trained Chinese nurses rose to the occasion and greatly enjoyed having me under their thumbs for a while. My back was massaged in great style and my face washed, etc. etc., so that I was fully recovered when Mary returned.

The Story of Hao Chih-Mei

Nurse Hao Chih-Mei deserves a story to herself. Hao Chu-en and Hao Do-en, two sisters, first came to our notice as grubby little girls playing round the chapel gate at Shaoyang, where their father, an ex-paper-idol maker become Christian, was then church gatekeeper. The two girls were able to attend the mission primary school round the corner. They did well and were then sent on, with missionary money to pay their fees, to the Methodist girls' secondary school at Hanyang in Hupeh. Having finished schooling, they returned home. Do-en, the elder, was soon married off, but Chu-en, the younger, who had taken the 'school name' of Chih-Mei, started teaching in a Government school. By then also, their father had lost his church job due to dishonesty, and had either to rely on his daughters, return to his old job—which was not allowable for a Christian—or beg for his food. All this only came to our ears when we began to hear a class in the nearby Government school singing well-known Christian hymns each morning. Also, the young teacher began again to attend church.

Soon we were looking around for suitable girls to form the second class in our new nursing school. Chih-Mei at once put in an application for herself to study nursing. Knowing her family background and difficulties, I said 'No, you are already well qualified to teach, you have a good job and you can help your family. You should continue at teaching. I could not even accept your father's guarantee in his present position. We cannot take you.'

But she would take no refusal and went on to canvass Mrs Stanfield and Sister Maud, who took her side. Eventually, she was admitted to the new class, but only after full explanation of the responsibility she was undertaking, and of the need not to follow in her father's ways. She had felt a real call to nursing, and that was that. Once she started she never looked back. Educationally she was far ahead of the rest of the class. In her ward work she soon showed herself to be one of those who is a 'born nurse'. In due time, four years, she graduated and almost automatically came on to the staff. The time came, when like other girls she married, her husband named Mung, being a secondary teacher at a city school. She went to reside in his home.

When her first baby was due she came to hospital and it was found that only Caesarian Section could save both herself and the baby. She agreed. The operation was performed and she did well. She now had her own little son. As she was recovering in the ward one day, she called to me: 'Now I know from experience what this hospital can do for a woman like myself. I am coming back to serve on your staff as soon as ever I can arrange my affairs.' And come back she did, with hardly a 'by your leave'! She engaged a woman to look after the babe while she herself was on duty. She was now 'Sister Tutor', able to teach and discipline the girls in a way that no English nurse ever could. She was irreplacable. A second baby was treated likewise.

When the Red Armies arrived she continued work as usual. Unrest and confusion were everywhere just then. One or two of the younger nurses had failed a recent exam, and in revenge, they made false charges against Hao Chih-Mei, to the new Communist police, who at that time were encouraging all and any complaints against anyone who had held authority. She was at once in great danger of arrest and imprisonment.

At dusk that evening she came to my home, telling Matron and myself the whole story. Knowing what was happening to so many at

90

that time, we could only agree to her immediate flight that very night before the police could get busy. I wrote out a short letter of recommendation to another hospital. Then, unknown to anyone else except her husband, she set out that night, on foot and alone, for the long walk across country to a new life.

Once there she was welcomed with open arms, though discreetly at first and possibly under a new name. She was soon as busy as ever doing her loved nursing work, and teaching nurses there too. Our loss was indeed their great gain. I do not doubt that but she still continues to serve her Master and her people.

Doctors

For my first years in Shaoyang I was medically alone. I used to say that I had hope that perhaps in fifty years our hospital might become a local institution supported locally and with its own Chinese national staff. I could not see it happening earlier, so many were the difficulties and changes ahead. In the event it was only thirty-one years later that I did actually hand the hospital to the local (Communist) authorities, with goodwill, as an active and running concern. Growth to this end was slow but continuous.

As work increased I needed help, and searched far and wide for a trained Chinese doctor to be my colleague. Not until 1927 did I find such a colleague, when a young doctor from Cheeloo Christian University came to us to take over during my furlough. It was a time of deep disturbance and confusion of mind amongst students. He did carry on but under him the hospital became simply a money-making concern. Staff prayers and ward services and free cases were discontinued and such was the general condition of the work that, before I returned, the Mission Chairman felt quite unable to continue to issue any further mission funds through his hands. Soon after my return the doctor announced that 'he thought he was in the wrong place'. He left and set up a private practice in the city nearby. Later he got into trouble through a case of aspirin poisoning and an injection case which went wrong. We then lost sight of him. Many years later he reappeared at our doors as a sad, sick and mentally affected tramp.

Doctor Li Chi-hsun

Searching for a successor, I finally got in touch with a Doctor Li, a St. John's University graduate from Shanghai. He was already in a lucrative private practice in Hankow, but a mutual friend thought he might be interested in a mission hospital appointment. I found

91

that he had been a Methodist scholarship boy at his college, but when he persisted in studying medicine instead of arts, as arranged by the mission, his scholarship lapsed, as did his mission contacts. In reply to my letter he decided to come to Shaoyang and look round. He came, he saw, and he stayed! He never went back to his practice. Instead he sent for wife and family to follow him, and together they took over the newly erected bungalow waiting for just such a staff member.

How glad he was, he told me, to get away from all the daily competition and money-seeking of what had been his Hankow practice, to a place where he could really use the skills that he had learned in Medical School. He was a skilled surgeon and became through the years an always trusted colleague. His wife, Hsu-Mei-Li, was to him a tower of strength. She had been headmistress of a school in Hankow. At Shaoyang she was always helping everybody and many a quarrel was settled in her home.

Doctor Li stayed with us for very many years, years of disturbance and difficulty, eventually getting a transfer to another hospital and thence into mobile Red Cross work. When the Red invasion came he was already back in mission work, working with Doctor H. T. Chiang at Hankow Methodist Hospital. It was while working there that he was proclaimed a 'Hero of Labour' by the Red Liberation Government, for the good work done with his patients. During the great flood of 1951, he had travelled to his hospital by boat along the flooded narrow streets, walked through deep water into the hospital, and at once started an emergency operation in all his wet and dirty clothes. This caught the popular imagination. During his time at Shaoyang, Li had had a year of special surgical study in England under a scheme whereby the Holt Steamship Company provided free passages (which I had had a hand in initiating).

Doctor Fu

This was a man who came to us as a graduate from Cheeloo University after one or two other appointments. He too, became a greatly trusted Christian colleague, and after some years was also able to get a year of study in England. Alas, while there he was found to have pulmonary tuberculosis, which interfered with his study, but good friends at home came to his help and he enjoyed hospital treatment under the N.H.S., got quite well and returned to duty in Shaoyang. He was always grateful for this experience, although not long before we left he had to sign a most scurrilous letter to the Methodist Missionary Society in London, cursing them and refusing to accept

92

any more of 'their dirty imperialist money'. This letter still exists in the files of the Mission in London. After Liberation, both he and his good wife were sent for long periods of re-education and indoctrination. But his good medical work continued.

Many other Chinese doctors served for shorter or longer times on our staff. Among these I must note the name of Doctor Tang-i-teh, the very first to get back to work after the Japanese evacuation. He got back long before I did. Also Doctor Chen Hsi-Min of Canton, later Senior Surgeon at one of the big Government hospitals in Hong Kong. Or there was Doctor Huang Chien, an F.R.C.S. of Belgium, Dr C. T. Yang, and Doctor Rynarchewski, a Jewish General Practitioner-refugee from Berlin, who was with us for some years. These and many others were all valued colleagues in the work.

CHAPTER TEN

Paying for it All

EVEN a small modern hospital uses money. When I first went to Shaoyang, apart from my own living allowance, the Methodist Mission provided a small annual subsidy, perhaps £250 a year for hospital expenses. This was a sort of foundation on which to build. In our early years it had to cover everything. If we spent more, that was up to me; I had to find it in advance. Our initial building costs were covered by a sum which had accumulated during the years when there was no doctor available. In later years we did begin to get occasional local subscriptions from richer Chinese patients, but as the work increased, the small sums which we charged to those who could pay became the major source of our hospital income.

Each year I had to make a full account of all monies received and spent, for the Mission. It is interesting to look back at some of these accounts. In my first financial year I find that we took the magnificent total of $12.00 Mex., worth about 18s. We were not getting rich quick. In those early years the increase was very slow, but the totals did increase every year. Many years later when we hit the currency collapse, the totals became astronomical. In 1946, just before the final collapse, we received and spent over twenty-five thousand million C.N.C. paper dollars in one year, and we needed a special accounting department to deal with it.

During all the years that I was there we never had any kind of Government grants, except that during my very last year the then Communist Government paid us a small 'Grant in Aid' towards the prevention of blindness work being done in our Eye Clinic, one of the very few such clinics in the country.

Through the years the Hospital Finance became an important side of my own work. We built up a small office staff, staffed by Chinese school teachers. They took most of the routine work from me. They said that I was 'the Finance Wizard' at the top.

It is worth noting that in our later years at Shaoyang (and apart from any emergency relief funds), each year over 95% of all monies received and spent was found locally in either fees or gifts. Yet from year to year we never had more than a microscopic balance in hand, but we were never in debt or overdrawn. We spent what we had. More was available when we needed it. The small Mission contribution made it all possible. Each shilling given did the work of a pound or more.

Squeeze. The Hospital Accounts Meeting

In those first years I was constantly having trouble from petty dishonesty. People seemed to feel that this English doctor was doing well and getting rich. Why should not they have a share too? It was our first qualified Chinese doctor, Doctor Hou Peh-feng, who casually suggested to me that the real trouble was that the money was all managed between myself and one other person only. 'Why not publicize all the accounts? Let them be seen by everyone.' He left, but his suggestion worked.

I therefore began our 'Accounts Meeting'. Each Friday evening I called to my study all the salaried staff, plus representatives of the nurse-students and the coolies. We opened with a simple prayer. The accounts for the week were then presented, each in duplicate, and signed by two staff members. The books were passed round to everyone in turn. There were books for In-patient fees, O.P.D. registrations, drug sales, kitchen accounts, X-ray fees, sundry purchases, etc. Everyone having seen the books, I asked if they were correct or if they had any questions to ask. Sometimes they had. Only when all were satisfied did I finally sign the accounts as correct. After the ice had thus been broken, we usually found quite a lot of hospital business to discuss together. Again and again very useful suggestions were made to improve service given, or showing how money might be saved. We always closed the meeting with a prayer, led by the Evangelist or one of the staff.

That routine having started, I never again had any serious trouble with petty dishonesty or graft. Everyone knew that this hospital was not a private money-making concern, but that we were all partners together serving the public and our church. It led to a most happy relationship amongst us. Each had his own fixed salary, though they would never pass round the salary list, preferring to avoid each other's curious gaze in that matter. I always felt that this little weekly meeting was a real Gospel witness, so successful was it in using even money to the glory of God, and in the daily to and fro of the business of what became a large institution.

Inflation

I am sometimes asked: 'What currency did you use in China?' That is a question more easily asked than answered. We began in the Old World of 1920. Copper cash coins were still in use, threaded in long strings in their thousands, and with a fluctuating value due to moves in the copper market. In the 1914 war the Japanese bought up most of this copper cash to make munitions. China then minted new smaller coins of higher nominal value instead. There was also pure silver available by weight and fineness and in Mexican dollars. These coins were mined and minted at the silver mines in Mexico and were valued for their reliability. China later minted silver dollars of the same size and weight, but when receiving change it was always necessary to 'ring' each individual coin. A coin with a dull sound was not pure silver.

During the days of the War Lords and on under Chiang Kai-shek, good silver gradually disappeared and was replaced by many types of paper notes which constantly depreciated in value. Runaway inflation reached its worst points before and after the Japanese invasion of 1944/5 and before the Communist take-over in 1949. To take just a few actual figures from our published accounts:

In 1942 we used of the paper C.N.C. dollars 465,000.00. By 1946 we used C.N.C. 17,812,000.00. By 1948 we needed C.N.C. dollars 25,659,004,000.00, to do the same amount of work. Then came the collapse. Silver returned clandestinely into circulation, together with all sorts of paper currencies. The real value of goods changed every day. No one knew what he possessed. This continued for months, until the Communist occupation, when they introduced their new currency, with very heavy taxation and strenuous efforts to restore stability. They have since maintained it at fixed rates.

During these years it was a constant anxiety how to live and how to pay a living wage to all our staff of ninety or more people each month. It really became a matter of faith. Salaries fixed for one month were quite impossible next month. Eventually we worked out a system. We would pay wages fortnightly. I started keeping a small personal index of prices so that I could see what the situation was. I found that the American Presbyterian Hospital at Siangtan was doing the same, and we compared notes. I talked over the whole situation each week at our weekly accounts meeting, and together we worked out a plan. On the day before each fortnightly payment was due, the staff would send out their own deputation into town to price six or eight leading fixed-quality goods, such as rice, or common cloth or a postage stamp. This was then the basis of an index from which the office staff could work out, by an arbitary fixed formula, the amount of currency needed that day to buy one nominal silver dollar's worth of goods. Next morning we paid out at that rate. Charges to patients went up at that same rate that same morning.

To make this possible we had to give up banking our daily takings. In the bank it only depreciated. Instead, at the end of each day our business manager used all available currency to buy whole pieces or bolts of cloth, which we stored in our empty granary until it was almost full. On payday we sold in the market enough cloth to get currency, or staff could take their pay in cloth if preferred. All this needed a tremendous amount of willing co-operation from everyone, but it was willingly given. We were a Christian team working together.

The Reds Approve

There is a final word to this inflation story. After the Communist Occupation or 'Liberation', every one of our coolies was minutely questioned by the new organizers. How much had they received? Had they been oppressed? All the story was told. We had actually managed to maintain our rates of pay slightly above market rates. The Reds gave us a good mark. It was recognized that the poorest staff had been treated fairly in these very difficult conditions. But they discovered that in the cases of three or four men we had for a time paid less than market rates. This was true, because in each case these individuals had come to us as helpless, dying men. They had been treated free and later given part-time work as a rehabilitation measure, gradually coming onto the staff as full-time paid workers. One of these had since risen to be head cook. All these coolies were instructed by the Red investigator to demand their 'full back pay' from me personally. Some of them did so and I had to pay. The cook however, refused to collect his back pay from me. As we were then waiting to leave for home and as we were not allowed to leave until all claims had been met, I sent for him to come to see me. Repeatedly he did not come. Finally he came. 'Doctor Pearson,' he said to me in Chinese, 'I am just ashamed to come to you and ask for this money. I don't want it. I know what you and this hospital did for me and I am grateful. I am well and able to work.' I replied: 'But I must ask you to take the money, or I can't go home.' 'All right,' was his reply, 'give it to me and I will take it and show it to *them*, and then bring it back to you.'

I paid it over and he left, but the Reds made sure that he had no opportunity to bring it back, for there would be all sorts of taxes and dues to pay after such a haul. He was not his own boss. All the same, I am still grateful to him for those words.

It was in September 1950, after a whole year of 'Liberation' and propaganda, that our hospital staff one day produced to us a 'A United Proclamation (or testimonial) to Our Beloved Doctor

97

Pearson', hoping that he and his wife would not think of going away on furlough for at least two years, and that Miss Hughes would stay with them for many more years. So, it is not true, even after all this agitation and indoctrination, that the people do want all foreigners to get out! It was good to know that we were thus wanted, but we had to explain that we had home claims as well, and we could not then foresee later developments. In effect we did stay another year.

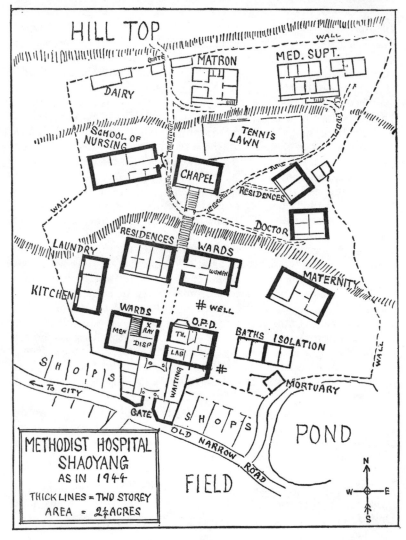

CHAPTER ELEVEN

Pioneers of the Church in Hunan

THE FIRST Methodist missionary to settle in Central China was Josiah Cox, who reached Hankow in 1861. David Hill joined him in 1864, just after the Taiping rebellion. Missionaries were soon working in many provinces, but Hunan remained proudly closed to them all. The rulers of Hunan set out to keep their loved homeland free from foreigners and all their works.

As the numbers of Chinese Christians in other parts of China increased, the Christians themselves came to feel a concern for the 'closed province'. In 1893 the Chinese Church at Teh-ngan in Hupeh sent two of its own members into Hunan selling Bibles and tracts. The following year E. C. Cooper, then a young Evangelist, made a lightning trip from Hupeh into Hunan, but he could not stay. Warren, North, Watson and others were likewise unable to gain a foothold.

In 1900-1901 came the great Boxer Rising, when all Christian work was disrupted and many missionaries and Chinese Christians were killed. It was not long after the suppression of the Boxers that G. G. Warren was able to get into Changsha, the capital of Hunan, and to stay there. (Though whenever he went abroad he was always 'protected' by an official, old-style, military guard.) E. C. Cooper and W. W. Gibson joined him in 1902. Warren remained in his base in Changsha but Cooper and Gibson were sent to South Hunan, in the first place to Paoking (Shaoyang). Later Cooper moved on to Yungchow (Lingling).

For years after his arrival Gibson spent his time, often alone, walking, walking, walking (like Mao Tse Tung later on) round the villages and townlets of the area. He would sit down and talk to whoever would listen, perhaps a shopkeeper in his open-fronted shop, or a passing farmer, breaking down prejudices or selling a gospel where he could. As his base he had only a noisy rented shop in the city to live in. Not till some years later was he able to buy from the Mahomedan Ma family, an old family temple, the very first property ever sold to our mission in Hunan. This was a great help. It allowed him some peace and quiet. On it he built a small chapel; it had two big doors opening on to the busy street. He would open the doors and start to sing or preach and soon had the place full of curious listeners.

On his many travels Gibson would never use a Chinese sedan chair. He preferred to walk and could easily keep up with the coolies' thirty miles a day. Before entering the ministry he had trained as a lawyer. He was hardworking and conscientious, always dependable.

G. G. Warren was the first Chairman and the great pioneer of Hunan Methodism. A very forceful character, he was one of the older generation who tended to lay down the law and to see that it was kept. His fluent Chinese always retained a curious Devonshire accent, and he said just what he thought. He expected young missionaries to do as they were told, yet he was a most lovable man and his Chinese colleagues had a great regard for him.

He was fearless in rebuking evil if he saw it, and on one occasion he personally accused the reigning War-lord, Governor Chao Heng-Ti, of having ordered the torture of a Christian teacher who had been arrested and killed for 'revolutionary thinking'. For any Chinese at that time, to mention such a thing would have meant instant arrest and execution.

In those days of disorder Warren was the only man they could find who could be trusted to hold the funds of the newly founded Chinese Red Cross Society. As treasurer he carried on his person a special pass from the Governor, allowing him in and out of the city gates at any time of day or night.

In his day he had been an athlete and was still a very strong swimmer. He swam the Yangtse at Hankow, almost losing his life investigating the dangerous whirlpools and cross-currents, and he swam almost round the mile-long island in the River Siang at Changsha. When he died in January 1927, he was still on duty in Changsha, despite prolonged sickness and revolutionary disorders and strikes against foreigners. He was buried in the local Christian cemetery. No striker thought of interfering with his funeral; he was too well-known and respected. I was at his graveside that day.

We Meet G. G. Warren

Mary and I, with baby Christine, first reached Changsha in January 1920, travelling by river steamer from Shanghai and Hankow. It was almost dark when our steamer tied up and we had been told to stay on board until next morning. However, we soon saw 'G. G. W.' in the crowd of noisy, gesticulating coolies on the landing stage, signalling us to come ashore. We did so. He led us straight up to the massive locked city gate, the Hsi Men, pushed his little coin-like token-pass under the gate for the guard to see and the gate opened as if by magic. We were soon happily at home in the old mission house at Hsi Chang Kai. Only a bare twenty years earlier Changsha

100

had been absolutely closed to every European. Warren himself had been one of the very first missionaries to enter Changsha 'freely, on foot, and in "foreign" dress' in 1900.

That same morning he had arrived back in Changsha from a visit as Honorary Chaplain to the Army of the Christian General, Feng Yu-hsiang, then stationed in Changteh in North West Hunan. While there he had baptized in one day 400 men! Those were the days. 'G. G.' and Feng were firm friends.

Years afterwards, when Feng was Assistant Commander-in-Chief of all the Chinese armies fighting Japan, he turned up one day in Shaoyang to review his troops. After taking the salute he called in at our hospital. He was overjoyed to find G. G. Warren's daughter Kathie, then living and working in Shaoyang. 'She is like my own daughter,' were his words. Having cast aside his Field Marshal's cloak, Feng left us, as was his wont, in his coolie clothes with his coolie carry-pole over his shoulder.

W. W. Gibson followed Warren as Chairman for some years. He was able to weld a group of enthusiastic English and Chinese younger colleagues into a wonderful team. He was still a pioneer working for the future. Following Gibson as Chairman we had several short-term appointments, all of them very fine men, but the circumstances of those days—things like civil war, revolutions, floods, sickness or family needs, caused a rapid turnover. Such men were William H. Pillow, John H. Stanfield, Cyril G. Baker and C. V. Cook. They were followed by the Chinese Chairman, Lai I-Hsioh and others. Stanfield, Baker and Cook all worked in Shaoyang and are still with us as I write. I have perhaps, deliberately refrained from bringing them into my story, but they are all very much a part of it and of our life during those years in Hunan. What wonderful colleagues they all were during those disturbed years! We were such a happy team, though we often had quite different places in the field. Cliff Cook, though a minister, actually took over the hospital superintendency during my furlough in 1938/39 and found it a great change from his usual church work. I think he quite enjoyed it.

The Synod Story

'Synod' was the chief executive body of the Methodist Church in Hunan. In our first year, 1920, the Synod met in Changsha, seated comfortably round the dining table of its Chairman, G. G. Warren. All except one of its members were English missionaries; English was its only language. The one Chinese present was the Rev. Wu I-tang, an elderly man recently ordained and he understood not one word of

English. When a vote was taken, the missionary sitting next to him would dig an elbow into the old man's ribs and tell him to hold up his hand to vote. That was the total of Chinese participation in the Church of those days.

About 1925 the big decision was taken that Chinese must be the only language of the Synod, both for debate and for the records. Newly arrived missionaries must learn the language if they would take part. If thus became possible for Chinese Christians to attend and take their full part in everything. Soon one or two younger Chinese ministers were ordained and lay stewards were appointed from each circuit to attend and to vote.

These years of development were constantly years of disorder and of civil war, the time of the War-Lords. There were disastrous floods and city fires. Sometimes it was quite impossible for Synod to get together. Despite all, each time that Synod met we saw a gradual increase in Chinese membership, until in 1946, we realized that in Synod there was now a voting majority of Chinese Christians. The missionaries were outnumbered.

But the church still leaned heavily on overseas financial support. Many were the efforts made to make it both independent and self-supporting. Most members, it seemed, were just too poor, living constantly on the verge of starvation. They were quite unable to support their own ministry, even at the very modest rates fixed by themselves in Synod. Even in 1949, 80 to 90 per cent of church funds were still coming from M.M.S. in London.

This impasse was never solved until, in 1950, the Communists did it for us! They simply forbade any Chinese church to receive any sort of subvention from abroad and at the same time the churches were compelled to write and sign most unkind letters to their missionary societies, refusing to accept any more of 'your dirty Imperialist money'. This took away overnight almost all the salaries of Chinese ministers and preachers.

Apart from finance, devolution of control proceeded smoothly. In all these years there was never a racial cross-vote in Synod . . . except once. For some years the elected Chairman of Synod continued to be a missionary, but when there were already six or eight ordained Chinese ministers of ability and experience, it was proposed that the senior Chinese minister be elected Chairman. Only the missionaries voted for the Chinese candidate; Mr Baker was elected by the Chinese majority. Two years later, the matter came up again, and this time Rev. Lai I-Hsioh was unanimously elected to the post. This all occurred before the Communist invasion so that, when that came,

102

it found a church in Hunan fully in the hands of Chinese Nationals. By that time a Chinese minister was already in the chair.

The Synod of 1950 was the last which I was able to attend. While the meetings were in progress each member of the Synod was sent for by the police and individually interrogated. They wanted to be sure that there was no Imperialist spy-work going on! During my own interview I managed to turn the conversation on to British politics and economics, telling them something of the British Labour Party and about death duties, etc. They were most interested and actually shook hands as Mary and I left, an unprecedented and unrepeated courtesy.

In 1951 police control was even more strict. No delegate could travel to Changsha without a special pass, and no passes were issued to non-Chinese delegates. That left a full Synod composed entirely of its Chinese members. It met, and business was transacted as usual. Thus it was that a truly Chinese Methodist Church was born. There is still a living Chinese Church in Hunan. How we thanked God for all the ways in which He had led us.

The Chinese Leadership

Among the early ordained Chinese ministers in Hunan was Rev. Tan Chen-ching, a Hunanese Christian who must ever be remembered. Mr Tan began life as a skilled lacquer worker in his native town. He listened to what was said by passing missionaries, and in middle-age he became a keen practising Christian. He was soon accompanying the missionaries and helping in many ways. Almost in his old age he was ordained as a minister and took charge of the church in his own home town of Liuyang.

One day, perhaps in the early 'thirties, a roving Communist army captured the town. It was in the days when the Communists considered any Christian to be a declared enemy of themselves. Tan and others were at once arrested and put up on a platform before a huge mob of townspeople and soldiers in the local open-air theatre. They were told to renounce their faith before the crowd—or else . . . ! In such circumstances that was a threat to life, and one or two weakly said what was required. But not so Mr Tan. Standing up before the crowd he spoke out: 'I am a Christian, but I am no traitor or "running dog" of the foreigners. I love my country and I believe that this is the best way that I can help China. I am a Christian and I can be no other. You may kill me if you like but you cannot hurt my spirit.'

At this a voice at the back of the crowd was heard shouting: 'This is a good man, you must not hurt him.' And in the resulting

103

confusion he was allowed to get down and go home. He remained in Liuyang and continued to minister to his congregation, until three years later he died of pneumonia while on a visit to some of his country members.

In this country J. H. Stanfield still has Mr Tan's own written account of the above happenings.

Other Friends

One of Mr Stanfield's first helpers in the church work at Shaoyang after our arrival, was a certain Mr Tai Chang-ching, a faithful but pedestrian Christian from Siangyin. When he was preaching he had a habit of repeating a certain phrase 'Na-ko-shih-hou' over and over again. It meant 'at that time' or 'then'. I used to try to count the number of times he said it in one sermon. I last met him when he was an old age pensioner of seventy-three—very old for a Chinese—and had then long left any paid service in the church. He was living in his old country home and was very busy organizing the church there and doing a bit of work that was outstanding in surrounding farms. One Saturday evening when I visited him, he was busy instructing some of his members to prepare themselves for Communion. 'Clean yourselves up,' he said, 'have a bath, and if you can't do that at least wash your feet before you come.' (No country village home has a bathroom, only a shallow wooden tub on the kitchen floor.)

This incident reminds me of what our last Chinese Chairman gave as his advice to his people bringing their harvest gifts to the church: 'Don't be like some folk who bring their dirtiest currency notes for the collection. In giving to God you must give your cleanest notes, not the dirty, old ones.'

The Rev. Lao Chang-nien was an outstanding man. He had trained as a school-teacher under Rev. B. B. Chapman, a former Rhodes scholar. Despite severe myopia he was so brilliant at college that after graduation he was retained for post-graduate training as an Inspector of Schools. He returned to Hunan to supervise all Methodist schools. While still a layman he became secretary to Synod. From this position, already at the centre of his church's work, he became a candidate for the ministry and in due time was ordained. He was a man of real intellectual power and of independent thought and a convinced Christian. He never hesitated to speak his mind as I found when I clashed with him once in Synod. We were soon on good terms again.

This was the man who, when we missionaries were leaving Hunan, was on the spot and already in the Chair. I think that we all felt that,

104

humanly speaking, we could not be leaving things in better hands. Surely here was a man raised up for this very task. Just before we left he had also been elected by all the Christians in Changsha as their member of the new city council. He certainly had a tough assignment.

I would have loved to write more of the many friends whom we made in Shaoyang over the years, and especially of our church contacts, but space forbids. Yes, we did have real friends even despite my status in later years as Missionary head of what had become a large institution and the economic differences caused by my receipt of even a modest living allowance from the church in England. Perhaps I never attained to the all-in economic oneness with my friends which the Quaker, W. G. Sewell, describes so graphically in his book about these same years of change, which he spent as a Lecturer in the Christian University in Szechuan*. Nevertheless, over all the barriers, my friends were real friends.

There were people for instance like Pao Liang-tao, who began life as a village boy and who in our last years was minister in charge of the Shaoyang churches. As such he had a very difficult time in the months following Communist Liberation, for he was also a forward looking and patriotic Chinese. When he preached the police were often in his congregation taking notes and challenging him afterwards. 'It is hard to preach these days,' he said to me. Mary and I still attended his services, though I could no longer occupy the pulpit in the circumstances prevailing. It greatly rejoiced our hearts to hear how faithfully he was putting over to his congregation the great Christian truths.

One day the police called him aside for questioning. They asked: 'Is this church now an entirely Chinese organization?' 'Yes.' 'Are you still receiving any foreign funds?' 'No, none.' 'Oh,' said the policeman, 'how is it that I see those two old English people at the back of your church every Sunday? Are they not still in charge?' At this point the conversation was getting difficult for Mr Pao. A wrong answer and he could easily end up in prison. He replied quietly: 'You know, sir, that I am a Christian minister. It is my duty as such to persuade people to come to church. I cannot even turn a Capitalist or an Imperialist away.' He put it thus crudely to help their understanding. His answer was accepted. He was warned, but the services continued, and owing to his bravery we were able to continue to have this fellowship with our Chinese friends right up to the end. (I had the above details from a mutual friend.)

*I Stayed in China (Allen & Unwin, 1966).

105

Tsao Ying-kwang, was the first of our hospital Evangelists, a job which was often more like that of an almoner and patients' friend. He could sit around, talk to people, sell gospels, and do all the many necessary things which were nobody else's job. As quite a young man Tsao had worked with one of the early German missionaries of the C.I.M., Mr Kampmann, on his trails round the countryside.

Always of a volatile nature, he proved to be happy, keen and useful at his work, but he fell and lost his job time and time again, for he was like a child with money and could never keep out of debt. If he had money in hand he would give it away or spend it, without a second thought. Then he would come to me hopefully, expecting more when none was due. Money just ran through his fingers. His wife and children were left penniless. He never spent it on himself nor did he gamble. Again and again I had to warn him until in the end we could no longer retain him on the staff. We were both of us very sad about this. He was a keen, bright, intelligent Christian, often attracting others to the Faith.

After a time in the wilderness he was back again in church service, this time in charge of a small village congregation at Fan-Chia-shan. He was still there when we left Shaoyang.

The Rev. Nieh Teh-chin began life as a policeman in Pingkiang, where he became a Christian. After years of faithful work as an Evangelist, he was ordained to the full ministry and I shall always remember him with gratitude. Two of his sermons remain with me in outline. In one he took up the question of whether a Christian must always tell the truth, as so many missionaries told him. He said that he felt that there are times when the 'blunt truth' is not the right word for a Christian to speak, for we must always love our neighbour and do what is best and kindest for him. That, for him, was Jesus' teaching on the matter. The other occasion was when he repeated over and over again the phrase of St. Paul, 'My grace is sufficient for thee'—'O-ti-en-tien-ko-ni-yung-ti'. I can never forget it.

Shao Tsu-chen

The Shaos were Shaoyang people. His ancestral home was in the north of the county near our mountain resort of Tung Kwang Ai. After schooling he went to Theological School and was ordained. After several pastorates we were very glad to welcome him back as Superintendent of the Methodist work in his own town, though we did occasionally find him 'difficult'. Mrs Shao was a trained teacher, a large hefty person, hard and self-centred, often a thorn in the side of her colleagues.

106

After the Japanese occupation and precipitate departure on VJ Day, 1945, Rev. Shao was one of the first church workers to get back to Shaoyang. As a Shaoyang man he knew the ropes. As minister in charge in the area suffering from acute post-war distress, he was soon being deluged with gifts of relief goods of all sorts, all greatly needed by people left destitute. It was to be many months before Mary and I were able to get back from England, in June, 1946. We arrived to find relief work in full swing. Powdered milk, flour, rice and tins of all sorts were being widely distributed under Mr Shao's superintendence.

He was soon pressing me to come into the relief work and to take over the vital treasureship from himself. I did this, but it was soon obvious, as in so many distributions, that things were not going too happily. About then several articles appeared in the local papers accusing him of lining his own nest. But nothing definite came out, certainly nothing that could justify suspension of a trusted colleague. His accounts were all in order so we carried on together while the first hectic stream of goods were distributed and the immediate needs met.

Then came the Communist Occupation of the town in 1949. Our new rulers had not been with us long before they picked up the whispers of scandal about Mr Shao. He was warned by a friend and got away before the Red police came for him. They therefore promptly arrested his wife and put her in prison until he or she should pay the large sum which they now said he had misappropriated. It also came out that he was also the owner of some quite valuable properties in town, of which we had never heard.

At this point the young Chinese deaconess working in the church in Shaoyang, comes into the picture. She took it upon herself to act as 'prisoner's friend' to Mrs Shao. As such she could get permission to visit the friendless prisoner and to talk to her as necessary. She took her Bible along and prayed with her there in the open prison yard. She was able to sell the town property and to raise sufficient money thereby, so that after fifty days she obtained Mrs Shao's release.

Mrs Shao returned to us a new woman, humble, kind and helpful. The sympathy, prayer and service given to her when she was down and out, together with all the Communist teaching she had to hear every day in prison, to the effect that she was a 'worthless old money-grubber' and 'a parasite on society' had made a real change in her. It was a case of real conversion, occurring there in that Communist prison. She realized that she was a sinner against both society and

God. Returning, she continued to live in her rooms at the church, but now, instead of making trouble, she wanted to help in every way possible. She took the place of the missionary's wife in Women's Meetings or primary school and was a wonderful comfort to Mary and I at the time of the big Accusation Meeting described elsewhere. A new Christian, converted in a Communist prison of all places!

Looking back it does not seem possible that what happened in Mr Shao's case was that he had considerable sums of money as well as goods passing through his hands. It was the time of the runaway currency depreciation. He kept all his accounts correctly, paying out the sums received weeks earlier. But, owing to depreciation, this might leave a handsome profit in his hands which would never show in the accounts! Something like this must have accounted for his troubles—and possibly for the property he had come by? He certainly did a lot of good relief work before and after I joined him in the work.

European Colleagues

Apart from the few pioneers already recorded, I have felt that it would be invidious, also not in accord with what I am trying to do, to give extended coverage to my many loved and trusted U.K. missionary fellow-workers, ministers, doctors and women workers. Even a list of their names would be long and tedious. At any one time there were usually ten to fifteen of us, plus wives and families, and usually someone either coming or going home. We lived scattered in distant centres, so that we rarely met unless at Synod or on holiday. A visitor who got as far as Shaoyang was a ten days wonder.

What a happy crowd we were. What a team, all glad to be able to live and witness to our faith amidst such wonderful Chinese people. Without such team work our task would have been endlessly difficult. With them, it was a joy.

We had excellent relationships with the Hungarian Franciscan Roman Catholic priests and nuns who worked in our city. One Mother Superior died in our home in Shaoyang, where she was being treated for typhus. At another time a certain Father Athanasius and I were the only Europeans left in town. How we used to enjoy getting together and singing some of the great multi-lingual Christian hymns! 'Venite Adoremus' was one, and he was particularly pleased to find one hymn in its Hungarian original in the S.C.M. hymnbook. Thus we found refreshment, but in those days before Good Pope John, we could not actually pray together.

Throughout the years we had close contacts with the German missionaries of the C.I.M. Associated 'Liebenzeller Mission', whose church was at the other end of our town. As Christian Fundamentalists they had their own ways and spoke what I learnt to call the 'C.I.M. language', in English as in Chinese. But even with these differences both sides learned to respect each other as true Christian comrades in a common work.

During the Second World War the German workers remained in China, though entirely cut off from their home base, and often without funds. After a time they were ordered into Chinese concentration camps unless their neutrality was guaranteed. My offer to give such a guarantee for the family working in Shaoyang, Rev. Kamphausen and family, was accepted on condition that they actually came to live in my own house for the duration. As I was alone, this was easy and they took over three rooms at one end of my bungalow as their home. This meant that they could continue their full work in their church as usual.

Both sides found rich benefits from the situation, but it gave rise to a lot of talk locally. One Chinese Christian commented: 'The English and the Germans are at war. This is just as though a Chinese family had taken a Japanese family into their home.' For these were the months when the dreaded Japanese Army was laying waste North China and making themselves so hated by their cruelty to the population.

Earlier during the same war Rev. A. Meyer, a German, used to come along to our Communion services, led by the Rev. Nieh Teh-chin, so that German and English were together led to the Throne of Grace by the Chinese Christian.

The Church in Shaoyang

The day in 1920 on which we and the Stanfield family first reached Shaoyang, we were welcomed a few miles outside the city by a small group of Christians who had come to escort us to our new home. They were then neither very numerous nor a very distinguished group. One schoolteacher, Mr Fan and his wife, one paid helper of Mr Gibson's, a few shopkeepers from the city, friends of Mr Gibson, but still living in their old-style non-Christian homes; and one old lady, Mrs O-Yang, who later came to act as chaperon at our first clinic. None of them great ones in this world, none rich and very few young people or women.

In his pioneer years at Shaoyang, Gibson had found the people unresponsive and often in great need physically. He had therefore appealed for medical help. In 1906, Doctor J. W. Pell had been sent to join him and start medical work. Alas, he was only able to stay for one winter as Mrs Pell was not able to stand the isolation and loneliness. They were moved to Hankow where he accomplished many years of wonderful work. In 1909 Doctor Heyward from Tasmania followed, but after three short winters he too was moved to the centre at Hankow, to help start the work of Medical Education. Before a successor could be found for Shaoyang, World War One intervened. I was appointed in 1916, but it was 1920 before Mary and I could reach China.

During our years at Shaoyang it often seemed that the growth of the church was very, very slow. As one looked around at a Sunday congregation the same few faces were present each time. Even among these few there would always be a few 'rice Christians'. Again and again the thought would come that there was no progress. Were we wasting our time?

It was only in later years, during the days and months of the civil wars, of Japanese bombing and the pressure of Red Indoctrination, that we saw first an increase in numbers, or, later under Communist rule, a decrease in numbers but the development of a small group of sincere and convinced Christians. On our last Sunday in Shaoyang there were at least thirty members ready and eager to stand up and take Communion. That meant a lot in those days.

The Growth of a Worker Ministry
After the Communist Liberation one of the Chinese Church's most urgent problems was the sudden drying up of all its overseas financial resources. Synod had relied heavily on Missionary funds. How could they support their ministry or even keep up their church buildings without these funds which they had been compelled to renounce?

The newly independent church set itself to meet the situation. Congregations did what they could, but all ministers had perforce, to look for some secular occupation. This was in line with Communist rule, that everyone must have a productive job—and preaching was not looked on as 'productive'. They might work six days in the week and be more or less free for church work on Sundays if other duties did not interfere.

In Shaoyang Mr Pao and the Deaconess together bought soap-boiling equipment and set up a small soap factory in the chapel vestry, using as their trade name 'Fu Yin Hwei Chao'—the 'Gospel

Soap Company'. It was this little company who gave us the final financial guarantee necessary before we could leave Shaoyang. I still treasure a piece of their 'Faith' brand soap.

Rev. Lao and his wife took over two or three cows from a missionary family, hoping to sell milk and thus stave off hunger while continuing to do their church job.

Others took jobs in teaching in the new Government schools—all schools get a holiday on Sundays, even in New China. Others undertook clerical work for six days a week. They had all felt a call to carry on, and had the will. 'Where there's a will, there's a way.' They were back into the early days of the church, before any paid ministry was evolved.

CHAPTER TWELVE

War and Relief

War. *The China-Japan Conflict reaches Hunan*

THIS WAR had been affecting the coast regions long before it reached us in Shaoyang. From 1936 on we found ourselves one of the places of refuge for people fleeing from the war. Well-to-do refugees crowded our town. Our hospital was in a position to give much needed medical aid. In July 1938, following the burning of Changsha, the Hunan capital, thousands of homeless wanderers came our way. Wounded soldiers were moved up country. Soon the Jap planes began to pay attention to such inland towns as ours. Their raids occurred mostly about midday due to distance from their bases and the need for daylight.

The Chinese worked out a system of raid warnings by long distance telephone. A first warning sent everyone scurrying out of town into the countryside. A second warning came as planes got near. At the hospital we did not move out but displayed Red Cross signs and Union Jacks to indicate what our buildings were, but we also had our trenches and encouraged all to take cover. Nurses' white uniforms had to be disregarded during raids as there had been machine gunning of crowds from the air, and white was much too conspicuous.

The first of these raids locally was in August 1938. The city authorities had asked the hospital to organize a First Aid squad and they provided 800 Mex. dollars (approx £70) towards stretchers, bandages, etc. The raid came on a stifling hot day. Our doctors and nurses at once went into action, going into the bombed streets to bring in the injured. The hospital was soon overflowing. Roman Catholic sisters at the other end of the town also helped. Together we reported over 300 casualties and perhaps fifty dead, but no accurate count was possible. That night panic reigned in the town. Rumour said that next day over forty planes would repeat the bombing. All night we could hear people leaving, tramping down the road, and next day the town was deserted and nearly all the shops closed, but no more planes were sighted for weeks. Gradually life resumed its normal flow.

Apparently it is always a first raid which creates this unreasoning terror. Later we learned to live with occasional small raids. Church services were changed from midday to late afternoons, at which time the danger was usually over.

The Japanese occupy Shaoyang

In the late spring of 1944, when the Japanese were getting nearer,

Portrait of the Author, in oils, by the Siamese artist
Dr Xien Kong-Kha-Kul. Painted aboard ship bound
for Hong Kong, 1963

Dining-room fireplace at Shaoyang, a water-colour
sketch by C. Mary Pearson

I was suddenly called to go home, as Mary was ill again in England. Of the journey I have spoken elsewhere. It was later that summer that the Japanese Army itself arrived in Shaoyang. Before I left it had been possible to arrange for Doctor F. McRae of the Church of Scotland to come to act as my locum. His own hospital was already occupied. He arrived soon after I left, but at once went down with typhus. He only recovered in time to retreat with all his staff in front of the advancing Japs. So dreaded were these Japanese soldiers that every person who could possibly move, left the town before they arrived; our staff moving in several parties into the mountains to the west. Those who then moved out included Doctors Li Chi-hsun, John Chen, Tang I-teh and nurses Chao Chih, Hu pei-chi, and others.

None of them was able to get back until some months after VJ Day, the first to arrive being Doctor Tang with Nurse Hu Pei-chi and party, who had remained round Wukang. They found the hospital occupied by Chinese military, having been completely looted by the local riff-raff after the Japs had retreated. My own bungalow had been burned down, the matron's bungalow had been destroyed by an American bomb and the rest of the hospital had been entirely cleaned out. Everything movable had gone, and not a door remained on its hinges or a pane of glass in the windows.

The returned staff got to work as and when they could. They got a few drugs from the Red Cross, they reclaimed various iron bedsteads and other furniture found in neighbouring houses and they got other relief supplies, etc., so that when I myself, was able to get back from England towards the end of the year, I found a busy hospital at work again. But it was months before all the losses of staff and equipment were made good, and the Nursing School at work as before.

After the Japanese Army left, the town was soon crowded with starving people. The fields had not been sown and it was too late to get any harvest. There was acute distress. Doctor Tang, Rev. Wang and others made the situation known, and long before I got back generous gifts for relief were coming in from many sources: UNRRA, CNRRA, American Red Cross, etc., all came to our aid. There were gifts of food, dried milk, drugs and medical supplies. A Red Cross gift reglazed all our glass-less windows. Friends at Greenfield, Oldham, rehabilitated our X-Ray, and many others helped.

The Chinese Christians in Shaoyang soon got busy. Rice kitchens for the foodless were opened, and run entirely by the church members as a voluntary service, something quite new in this part of the world.

113

A seldom used Taoist temple was borrowed. Soup tickets were distributed secretly at night to street sleepers to avoid almost certain crushing and loss of life. Each morning rice was cooked in the temple by women helpers, and all those possessing tickets were fed at noon. As the ticket holders arrived and were admitted, they sat down in rows in the temple, and while they waited other helpers brought along a stock of simple reading books and got busy teaching the women and children to read. Medical first-aid was also at hand from some of the hospital staff.

This was a most successful piece of relief work and it produced a feeling of *esprit-de-corps* among the Christian helpers which was very good to see.

Famine in Hunan

The Province of Hunan, with its two crops a year from much of the land and its warm, moist climate, is not the type of country often subject to food shortages or famine. Nevertheless, during our years in Hunan we experienced famine conditions several times. A flood during June or July, the rainy season, or a crop failure due to insect pests, resulted in many starving people next May, June and July as stores ran short and they waited for the new rice crop in August. Gross disorganization of the State by Civil wars or by Japanese invasion, caused widespread suffering to many of the poorest, for whom there was no help.

Our first experience of famine was as early as 1922, when the rice crop failed. The small wheat harvest next spring helped to delay the worst effects, but by June people were already leaving their fields to come and beg and die on the city streets. This was when we took the orphans into our newly-built wards as described earlier.

Seeing the need I got into touch with any available Relief Organization, and a considerable quantity of Kaoliang (millet) was sent up, which I was asked to distribute personally. This proved most difficult. We had to store it in the empty public granaries, and I personally stood in the granary watching every load come in or go out. Even with such close supervision it proved impossible to be sure of a just distribution to the real poor. Wealthy men would nominate their own relatives as recipients and in many ways I am sure the grain got into wrong hands, though it did increase the total quantity of food available. How similar it was to the great Potato Famine in Ireland in 1846.

As distress continued into 1923 I next wrote to the newly formed United Relief Committee in Changsha, informing them of our local needs, and telling of my own recent experiences in Russia. I felt that it was necessary to provide work for the poorest. There was still food obtainable if they could earn money to buy. The most obvious need was the construction of new roads for motor traffic. At that time the old foot-paths with steps up and down were still our only roads. Earth moving can be wonderful relief work, and the most important construction needed at that time was a road to cross the main watershed of the Province from Siangtan to Shaoyang. My letter was read to the Committee and was at once taken up by them as a major project, using mostly American Red Cross funds, and with provincial Government co-operation. A rapid survey was made, Chinese engineers were engaged and quite soon they were ready for workers. I found myself Chief Labour Recruiting officer at the Shaoyang end of the line, and also local paymaster. I had to find and organize the labourers into gangs of twenty, who then elected a Head Man from amongst themselves. We soon had all the men we could use. I kept all names and addresses and each man might designate his wife or a relative to collect part of his pay each week from me. This worked well and was much appreciated.

As soon as famine conditions were over, Government stepped in and completed the road work by the construction of good stone bridges. I always felt a bit possessive when in future years, I often passed along that road.

1924 brought another disaster following the great flood of that summer. That time I have no record of outside relief, but my hands were very full trying to get our own hospital reconstructed and working again. We provided work on building that winter.

In 1937 we started a scheme to train village Health Workers, who would learn to use a few simple remedies and First Aid and continue to live in their villages. They were also vaccinators. All who graduated were provided with a small First Aid Box with instructions, and were told that they might replenish their stocks from time to time from hospital at fixed prices, profiteering would be frowned on.

Farmers' Co-operatives

In 1947 I was again busy with a scheme to help farmers hit by flood and famine. Using International Relief Committee funds, we organized twenty-one small Farmers' Co-operatives in one village area. Each little society was to have ten members. When all were registered and organized and mutually guaranteed, each man was loaned one load (about one hundredweight) of seed rice at sowing time. This would keep him out of the hands of the money-lenders

115

and he was expected to repay his loan in kind at harvest. The work should thus be self-perpetuating. Alas, the general disorganization of society did not make a scheme like this easy to work, almost fool-proof though it was, and we lost much of the capital. I was interested to learn during the Red Occupation that something was still going on with official approval.

I meet Kagawa

In 1938, going home on furlough and travelling alone, I arrived in Hong Kong one morning prepared for a wait until I could get a steamer passage for London. At lunch I noticed that there was a Japanese steamer in port which had on board the Japanese Dele-gation to the World Missionary Conference shortly to take place at Tambaram, Madras. Kagawa was one of the delegates. I at once got busy with the shipping offices, did a double-quick turn round with my bags, got a tourist passage and a special launch out into the harbour and was aboard just as the S.S. *Fushimi Maru* was lifting her anchor.

I then found that all the Madras Delegation had been put into the First Class as a special compliment by the shipping company. We could, however, talk freely on deck, and I was able to get to know both Bishop Mann of the Methodist (U.S.A.) Church and Toyohiko Kagawa himself, the great Japanese saint. This was the period when Kagawa's difficulties with his own Government were at their height, for Japan was at war with China. I was warned by his missionary colleagues to be specially careful not to get him into trouble with his authorities by careless speech.

He and I nevertheless found plenty of opportunity to walk round the deck, or to stand in the bows of the boat where the wind is strongest. There we could talk without any possibility of being over-heard. He was quite blind in one eye and had only half-vision or less, in the other, due to old trachoma and ulceration.

I used the opportunity to ask him about the peasant farmers' Co-operatives, which we had been trying to start as a relief measure in China, but which always seemed to come to grief because the peasants were never sure of making the repayment of their loans after harvest. What was the solution? How could we make these co-ops. work? What was his experience in doing just this kind of work with Japanese peasants?

He paused for a minute as the wind blew past us. Then he said two words: 'Four eggs'. 'Four eggs?' I repeated. 'What does that mean?' Slowly he explained. 'Every Chinese farmer I expect, keeps

116

chickens? Do Chinese hens lay eggs like Japanese hens? Get your Chinese farmer to set aside four eggs out of every ten that his chickens lay and take them to the co-op. That way the co-op funds will accumulate and he will regard them as his own hard-earned money. He will see that it is carefully used and repaid on time.'

'Self-help' was thus to be the solution. 'Big funds sent from abroad can never be the same. A poor man will just drink them up as they fall from the skies, and wait for more. Occasionally much larger funds can be used in an acute emergency, as Inter-Church Aid has been able to use them, but if these gifts are continued they can produce a situation which may seem quite hopeless, as with the Arab refugees in Palestine, still dependent on United Nations charity.'

Kagawa also told me of some of his difficulties in Japan, due to his opposition to then militant Nationalism and Emperor worship. 'Anyone suspected of unusual thoughts is regularly spied upon or imprisoned. Police attend all church meetings. Recently one "new religion" had been entirely suppressed. The Roman Church had given way about Emperor-worship for its members, saying "it is not a religion". 'I cannot publish these things', Kagawa told me, 'even at the coming Madras Conference. When the writers come to me I am dumb, but we do pass them from mouth to mouth. I do not think that Japan wanted this war, she wanted to keep Russia out of Manchuria. Chiang Kai-shek resented this and he was too strong, so now Japan finds herself fighting China instead of Russia. We need an International Police Court. Japan cannot win this war, China cannot win . . . (pause) but the Church can win! Recently our Prime Minister, Prince Konoye, broadcast to all Japan telling of the wonderful work of Christian missions and hospitals in China as seen by the Japanese armies. Our armies will give all facilities for such work and this will also help Christians in Japan. As to our Christian missionaries in China, you must just stay on your jobs during these days of war. Tell your friends not to talk politics, but to get on with their work. There will be a wonderful opportunity for the Church in China in the coming days.'

Red Army Wounded

Our last efforts at Relief Work were in 1949, during and after the Red invasion and 'Liberation'.

Before the Army arrived we had picked up a lot of severely wounded Red soldiers from the city streets and put them in our wards. When they did arrive as victors they found every available bed filled by their own men, happy and loud in their praises for nurses and doctors. They told us to 'carry on'. We had won the first round in the battle to gain their confidence.

Shortly afterwards the Red wounded were all transferred to their own military hospital, their expenses having been met by their officers. But now we discovered a whole party of defeated Chiang-Kai-shek troops lying untended in a dirty, disused temple nearby. We began to visit and to help these and some Christians sent the food. But the Reds stepped in and told us 'It is never right to help any enemy of the people', and ordered us to stop it all. After that we had to help them by stealth.

Agricultural Adventures

When Mary and I first reached Shaoyang we could get no fresh milk. There was none, though every other farmer had his working cow or buffalo. For our family, therefore, we brought in tinned milk and other imported foods. Before long, Christine was down with scurvy, and something had to be done. I bought a local cow and taught a local man how to milk it, and it gave us just one pint a day. But how valuable that was. From then on I always tried to maintain at least one or two cattle for our milk.

A Cow by Passenger Train

Some years later I was able to get a half-bred Jersey heifer in calf from an Agricultural Mission in North China. Bringing it to Shaoyang was another matter. It had to walk to a railhead—twice over because there was a minor war in progress—eventually it reached Hankow and I sent my old cowman to collect it. He had difficulty in crossing the Yangtse with it in a small row-boat, but he got men to both pull and push behind to get it aboard. Then it had to get a train to Changsha. There were no cattle trucks or wagons available, so he actually put it into a passenger wagon, and was very annoyed when the ticket man demanded two fares for it saying: 'It has four legs, hasn't it?' However, it reached Changsha. Owing to the many delays it was now midwinter and he started to march it the last 150 miles. That was before the motor road was built; he made perhaps ten or fifteen miles a day if the going was good. But soon the cow failed and could go no further. It slumped on to the mud floor of an inn, cold and tired and hungry. He thought he had lost it. But he bought straw and lit a fire on both sides of the cow and poured some local wine down her throat, and presently she began to raise her drooping ears and come to life! He got her to Changsha alive and for many years she was a great treasure—'Daisy', we called her. She later became a case of true epilepsy and gave us more adventures, but she was a wonderful milker.   And what a boon her milk was to our children and also to hospital patients with a like need.

Time and time again we suffered the loss of cattle due to infectious disease, rhinderpest and infectious pneumonia, but each time I was able to save one or two animals by strict isolation, and so we carried on until the Jap invasion, when all were lost in the fighting. But even after that we got going again with the help of the Mennonite Mission in China, who imported a lot of cattle to restock Chinese farms. They donated four heifers and a bull from U.S.A. to us, and actually delivered them to our door by truck!

Only in our later years was I able to obtain vaccines from a Chinese Government Institute in an attempt to mitigate our always recurring losses.   There were still several beasts on the hospital staff when we handed over to the New Administration in 1951.   I expect they would soon be transferred to one of their new Agricultural stations.

Bee-keeping

This was another thing that I learned in China. It started when a Chinese friend, Mr Ho, one day presented me with a swarm in a box, and I had to ask what to do next. As with the dairying I had to start from scratch, and then to send for books on the subject and read it up. From keeping my first bees in an old packing case, I finished by having them doing good work in the latest modern beehives. In our last year in Shaoyang, when sugar was almost unobtainable, my one hive of bees presented us with seventy pounds of wonderful honey! My first bees were of a local black strain and were very subject to attacks by wax moths. Later I got an Italian strain which somehow kept the moths under control itself.

On the vacant bits of our hospital site I tried to introduce new and improved varieties of cotton, a great improvement on the type of cotton grown by local farmers. Oranges too, interested me. Having got a few pips from very good oranges, I grew them for twenty years before getting a harvest.   My Chinese friends told me it was all wrong and I could never get fruit. But when I got two hundredweight of the finest fruits in the famine year, they were soon coming and asking for cuttings from my trees!

CHAPTER THIRTEEN

Over Hill and Dale
China—Japan Wartime Travel

FOR OUR LAST decade at Shaoyang we were served by the completed motor road to Changsha which eliminated the old sedan chairs. During the few years before the Japanese invasion the new roads were at their best. Also the Hankow-Changsha-Canton Railway had been completed and was working and other lines were under construction. Travel was cheap, easy, and always crowded.

It was when the Japanese armies began to move inland that troubles began. All petrol supplies disappeared. In its place Chinese ingenuity installed charcoal-burner stoves on the buses. These, with the addition of a little water, produced methane gas which could run the petrol engine. It only gave reduced power, but for some years it kept the old buses running, even into the last stages of decay.

As the Japanese forces advanced, the Chinese Government ordered the literal destruction of all threatened roads or railways. All embankments were ruthlessly dug up and bridges destroyed. Even the old-style footpath roads were similarly treated. Travel anywhere could now be exciting, as well as frustrating. Especially as travellers might easily become targets for Japanese airborne machine gunners, or the local highwaymen.

When the roads were open there were never enough of the Government sponsored buses running. Private traffic was not allowed. The biggest difficulty was often to get a bus ticket to allow one to travel at all.

One afternoon in 1944, I went round to the Shaoyang bus station to register my name for a ticket next day. I was told to come early as the bus would start at dawn. I duly arrived, but the officials were still asleep. Presently two clerks awoke, got into a sort of pulpit in one corner of the waiting room and called out the names of the people who had registered as wishing to travel. If they were present and answered to their names, each was given a small wooden tally entitling him to queue at the ticket office for a ticket. Tickets having been purchased, one's luggage must be weighed and excess paid for. Finally one got a seat in the little bus, packed to its utmost limit with people and baggage. When all are safely inside, and if the door can be shut, probably the bus will start, or we may wait for another hour while it gets up steam or gas from the charcoal fire. Government passengers usually get a priority on these journeys, others just wait. I remember once buying a bus ticket at Changsha, when a whole queue

120

was just a scrum at the ticket window. I went head down in the approved Rugby manner and got my ticket!

A Letter

In January 1943, I had been attending Synod at Changsha and in a letter to Philip described my return journey to Shaoyang:

'Cliff Cook and myself left the Hsin-Ming-Tang chapel at 5 a.m. (breakfast was served at 4 a.m.).We had a mile-and-a-half walk across town to the riverside. We set off in the dark and in pouring rain. The streets were all mud and unlit, so one could not avoid the deep puddles. We had two rickshaws with us to bring the luggage. Apart from the rickshaw pullers we saw no-one till we were halfway across the town. A night-watchman was solemnly beating his gong to keep the thieves away. Only two weeks earlier the town was under curfew, when no one was allowed on the streets during the hours of darkness.

'At the riverside we could just make out the launch getting up steam, and also a lighter at the foot of a steep muddy bank. We made for the lighter, the launch itself being already crowded to capacity. We had been told that it held a First Class cabin with a roof on! Most passengers squat like sardines on the open deck. We were shown a small door in what looked like a small wardrobe, with two steps down inside it and a hole below. Our bags were unceremoniously pushed through this hole and disappeared from sight. We followed them into the "wardrobe".

'Inside all was dark. When we had had time to get adjusted to the lack of light, we found that we were in a small steerman's cabin, full up with people trying to turn in all directions at once. They made us welcome, told us to sit on an empty bunk and demanded our fare. We sat down and paid up. Our cabin had a mat roof and wooden shutters in place of windows. It was still dark as we got under way; but the coming of dawn made little difference, it being too cold to open the "windows". There now appeared to be about fifteen passengers in the space of a small railway compartment. Occasionally the steersman cleared a space around himself and moved the steering wheel a bit.

'After a time a charcoal brazier was brought in and set down on the floor. This was much appreciated. Most passengers seemed to be smoking local tobacco, soon the atmosphere was more like the Black Hole of Calcutta than anything. Next a member of the crew insinuated himself into the room and proceeded to sing us a long story in the old sing-song style. He then passed round the hat and was loud

121

in his complaints that his collection was only three dollars in small coins. A fiddler followed. He took up his collection in the open end of his Chinese bamboo fiddle. Next a ready-cooked Chinese meal appeared from nowhere—but we had our own buns and thermos. It was under these conditions that I tried to begin this letter. We endured six long hours before we reached Siangtan and could escape from our Black Hole.

'We next must find a train to Hengyang. First to a Chinese inn to get a meal of hot rice, after bargaining about its price. Then across the river to the railway station. We now found the "Express" starting, a fine, steel-built, corridor train, filled with well-dressed through passengers with fur coats and travelling rugs. One could hardly imagine a greater contrast to our last conveyance. Alas, a window has been smashed and all the wind and rain comes in.

'It was 8.30 p.m. and dark when we reached Hengyang station. There was no moon and still raining cats and dogs and we must cross the river to get to the city. We found two coolies to carry the baggage and set off to find our way to town. This walk included crossing the wide, Siang River by sampan (in the dark), climbing down and up its slippery mud banks, and across a single plank suspended over the water (our boots were then thick with slippery mud) to reach the sampan. On the city side I diverged to call at the American Mission Hospital, while Cliff went direct to an inn—all in the black darkness. I only knew the approximate whereabouts of the inn. Having paid my call I went out to try to find Cliff. Strangely enough the very first door I went in at was the right one. I could rest and get dry again. I felt that that was just another piece of guidance. Next morning was to be our bus ride to Shaoyang, 100 miles.

'Cliff was up first and went out to get the bus tickets. Again big crowds were trying to travel, and here no tickets are sold until a bus is ready to start. Then the scrum starts and buying a ticket is a strenuous job. In this case the station master recognized us and called us inside to get the tickets and we got our crowded seats in the bus. The bus is an old Ford truck with a local soft-wood body. Only the tiniest of seats, and luggage over and under everything. All ticket-holders are rammed in somehow. Not half an inch of space is left. In this case the bus was so full that the rear door would not shut and one man was compelled to alight and be left behind. Also one soldier, who had carefully got into a back seat without a ticket, was made to remove himself. His only way of exit was via the canvas-covered "window"—so out of the window he went, still protesting. The day was frosty with a bitter north wind, so we were all willing to keep the windows closed. Six more hours of this enforced darkness and we were once again in Shaoyang. On our arrival we were met by Ernest Wright and Miss Swann, who had left Changsha two days before us. They had taken a day longer on their trip; their bus had been held up by bandits. All the passengers were turned out and searched and all money and valuables taken from them. Ernest lost his new watch and Miss Swann her money and goloshes. Having got what they wanted the five men with their assorted rifles decamped to disappear into the countryside.

'Well, well, such is life. I do not really enjoy travel under these "modern" conditions. The sedan chairs and river junks were so much more peaceful. Hospital is busy as usual and Chinese New Year festivities are approaching when everyone who can goes home. I would not mind being at home with you all, too.'

Love to all,
Dad.

Through Vietnam to Hunan

The disorganization caused by the Japan war was the reason for much travel by unusual routes. Twice I travelled home via Siberia—but that was earlier. For a time Hong Kong was our port, reached by rail via Canton. Later we had to enter through Macao and cross the delta by junk to the Canton River, and then via the North River to Shaokuan, dodging Japanese bombers meanwhile. When that became a closed route in 1939, in order to get back to Hunan I had to travel via Haiphong (now North Vietnam) and thence by the French Mountain Railway to Kunming in Yunnan and thence via the Chinese end of the Burma Road to the far west borders of Hunan.

On the trip via Haiphong I had with me two newly appointed missionaries for Hunan; Hilda Hudson, a nurse, and Norman Pratt, a young minister and former agriculturist in Lancashire. On the French Railway we had opportunity to experience for ourselves something of the then hopelessly corrupt French Colonial regime, when almost every one of our trunks or cases was systematically broken open and robbed while under guard as registered luggage, on the train and despite all precautions. We did reach Kunming with some of our luggage, but no redress for what was missing.

At Kunming we could contact our own M.M.S. colleagues. They found us places on a long-distance bus to Kweiyang in Kweichow province. Our bus was the typical, tumbledown vehicle with the usual hard, crowded seats and all space filled with baggage of every

123

description.   It was to be a several days' trip, stopping overnight at roadside inns whenever the driver thought need. Meals were to be had at these inns, often cooked beforehand, 'on spec', by the inn-keeper. Lavatory accommodation on the road was our biggest problem, just the most primitive pits, behind or at one side of the inns. I had to go and explore and make a way for Hilda at each stop. All very embarrassing for a nurse just out from home for the first time. But she was game.

I have found a few notes written on this journey and now quote:

'Jany. 22, 1940. What a strange two days we have been through since leaving Kweiyang. We will always remember it. We started yesterday at 8 a.m. after brief English prayers in the inn by the roadside. The road took us up and down steep hillsides, through scenery which is enough to make any place famous for its wildness and beauty. Up and down high mountains we went, round hair-pin bends. One ascent needed 24 hair-pin bends before we were at the top. It was like going up a staircase by bus. At other times we were speeding along the edge of sheer precipices. These were the moun-tains of Kweichow. Our little bus contained eighteen people with all their baggage, but it took the gradients without pause or stop. At one small village we were halted for a passport examination by a military search party. We were O.K. but two of our fellow passengers were arrested and removed for carrying opium; all quietly and efficiently done.

'As we continued to climb, we began to see traces of hail or snow on the road. Soon all was white and the road inclined to be hard frozen and glassy, but we still went up and on. Suddenly on a steep incline near the top of a mountain called Pan-Shan, the bus engine failed, the driver lost control and we started to slip back on the icy road. Only after ten or twelve yards did the driver get his brakes to act and we stopped dead, just six inches from the edge of a very steep mountain edge, down which the bus might have rolled over and over very many times. Everyone at once got out, thankful to be alive, and stones were found and placed behind the wheels.

'Now the engine refused to start up. One or two passing buses stopped but could not help. It was already 3 p.m. I felt that in these wintry conditions it would be well to walk on and try to find shelter somewhere. Villages are few and very far-between in these moun-tains.

'We picked up what we could carry, including a rug each, our food bag and our overcoats. Hilda could not get at her overcoat so I dressed her in my woolly dressing gown. It fitted her exactly for the job and off we went. It proved a long walk and darkness overtook us. Presently a passing lorry gave us a lift, but ran past the village we were making for and a few miles later his power also failed on a steep muddy hill. We started to walk on again in the dark. On and on . . . Finally we came to two tiny roadside mud huts or "shops" and a larger house built to house road-working coolies. We were now nine walkers as others had joined us. The only two beds at the shop were already occupied by opium smokers, but the shopkeeper did get us a rough meal.

'It was now a bitter cold, freezing night. Mr Tseng, a friendly passenger, was able to find some straw, and with this, he and we all turned into the road coolies' hut, already well-filled with sleeping men, one of them with a very bad and frequent, noisy cough which went on all night. The rugs we had carried were now invaluable, and at any rate we were shut in from the bitter, icy wind. Hilda was a brick, making no complaints, curling up with her rug and my dressing gown and doing her best to sleep.

'Next morning we were all up with the lark, foot-slogging along the road to get warm. By 10 a.m. we reached a small town, San-Hwei, not far from the Hunan border, and found an inn. We had not been there long when all our luggage and bedding arrived on a passing lorry. No charge! We had left it dumped by the roadside in the mountains! A little later our bus appeared, only two days overdue. He stopped when he saw us and we took our seats as though nothing had happened. It is happenings like this that make me feel more at home in China. While we had been waiting I had been able to explore San Hwei. I visited a lonely Roman Catholic priest and found a Buddhist temple which, among its idols contained a tablet to "Shang Ti" the Christian God! Someone must have been trying to combine his religions.

'It was at another stop-over on this trip that we arrived at a small town, rather late. All the inns were full. We found a cafe where they would allow us to sleep on the tables. We had our blankets so were glad to accept. I had not long turned in when I became aware of curious and unusual noises not far from me. I switched on my torch. To my amazement I saw dozens of rats, large ones, on the table next to me where the assistant had left some dishes of food. As I shone the light on them the rats gradually scuttled away down the table legs, and peace reigned once more.

'Which story reminds me of another occasion at home in Shaoyang when I was awakened one night with a feeling of comfortable warmth at the top of my head. I moved and stretched up my hand, when a

125

large rat moved quietly off. He had found a nice warm nest for the night in my hair. He was caught and dealt with next day, but did you ever read of a comfortable rat before?

'But I digress.

'Next day we were at the Hunan border. Here we had to change buses and were soon off again along a very new road over the West Hunan mountain massif. How I stand amazed at these Chinese road-makers. Up and up the road goes. In and out and round, but always up over hill and dale. At times we seemed to be running along the very highest tongue of land in the world, the land sliding away into the mist on *both* sides of the road as still we mounted, up and up. Were we off into the sky in Elijah's chariot and horses? Still we went up. Again we reached snow, but this time it was melting and slushy. Dusk brought us to Huang Hsien, the first town in Hunan, where we found a modern-style China Travel Hotel. A further day of routine hard going and we were home in Shaoyang.'

Over the Hump

In May 1944 I was urgently called home by our mission as Mary, then in England, was said to be ill. No details were given, and the Japanese Navy had by then closed all normal roads out of China. It was still possible to fly out via India. I decided to use a new railway then being constructed through the mountains to reach Kunming. This involved going by bus to Hengyang. Then train to Liuchow in Kwang Hsi, and then north-west along a new line aiming at Kunming. This only took me as far as Tu Shan (Lone Mountain), an apt name. After a night there, I managed to buy a seat in a regular post office van. They were only allowed to take one passenger. The van itself was filled with the mail bags and we set off. Well outside the town limits we stopped and half a dozen willing passengers appeared from nowhere. This I found was the institution known as 'Yellow Fish'. The back of the van was opened, the bags rearranged, they each paid what the driver asked and got in. They all got out again before we reached the next town, so the van arrived all in good order. This driver was out to save money. To do this he always shut off his engine at the top of a steep hill and free-wheeled down, thus using less petrol. It certainly made for nightmarish riding down those mountain sides, strewn as they already were with numerous wrecks by the roadside.

By this route we often passed settlements of primitive Miao People, and stop-overs would give one a chance to walk round. One such stop was at the town of Chin-Kiang-Chen, 'City-of-the-Golden

River' where the swift flowing river did really shine like gold in the setting sun and where I got as a memento a small seal cut out of the local red and pink soapstone.

Having reached Kunming, I had next to look for air transport over the Himalayan foothills to India. Resident colleagues soon arranged this and I found myself a passenger on a small two-engined Chinese army plane returning to Calcutta for war supplies. The crew was all Chinese. Kunming is 6,000 feet above sea-level and it was very cold so I was still wearing my sheepskin coat and fur cap.

As we rose above the town we got a wonderful view of the country-side and lake, but as we rose higher and met a few air-pockets I began to feel uncomfortable. The plane was not pressurized and seats were arranged around the inside, army-fashion. Before long it was quite evident that most people were feeling like I was. Almost everyone was sick. The plane continued to rise and fall, and must have been about 12,000 feet up. I suppose we must have been suffering from cerebral anaemia. I just could not hold my head upright nor sit up and I felt that my safety belt was cutting me in two. I managed to loose the belt and slide on to the floor, semi-conscious. Most of the twenty odd other passengers did the same, and we just stayed quietly on the floor until the plane came to land at Ding-kiang airfield in North Assam. There they turned us all out and gave us a cup of coffee while they cleaned up the plane.

The second leg of our journey over level ground and in the dark, was uneventful and I duly arrived on a hot day in Calcutta in the tropics, wearing fur coat and hat. My first task after reaching our Mission House was to go out to the markets and get some sort of tropical clothing.

Perhaps I should add that one passenger did manage to maintain his seat on that journey. He was Doctor Lin Yu-tang, the author. Years afterwards I met him again in Hong Kong and reminded him of our adventure, which he remembered at once, 'Yes, that was in 1944,' he replied.

After a long delay in India finding a passage (it was wartime) I was home again and I found Mary just beginning to pull out of one of her worst times of depression. The family was more or less looking after itself as well as caring for mother. Christine was then a student nurse in Liverpool and Andrew a medical student with digs in Liverpool; Eleanor was a student, yet somehow little Frances was looked after. What a welcome I got. And before long Mary was her active self once again.

127

CHAPTER FOURTEEN

Mary's Part—Her Home

A Home in China

THE FIRST six months after Mary and I arrived in Hunan were given mostly to language study. We had a big empty house, next door to our Chairman, Rev. G. G. Warren, in Changsha. Housekeeping on her own was still a new adventure for Mary. She was appalled when she found that almost at once she was expected to house and feed six missionaries over the ten days of the Synod. One of the guests was to be Rev. E. P. Scholes, a very particular vegetarian with a reputation for asking awkward questions about the food set before him. He arrived late, but when he did come he was as good as gold.

For the hot weather season we were sent to the lovely hill station of Kuling in Kiangsi together with our language teacher, Mr Yang Hung-Yu. We had a small bungalow and looked forward to a happy time getting to know other missionaries, but when young Christine came out with a scarlet fever rash social functions were cut to a minimum, much to Mary's disappointment. The air at Kuling was delightfully cool, though the sun could be hot. The hill tops all around us were covered with wonderful greenery and flowers, azaleas, lilies, etc., and great trees around the old temples. Alas, travel from Hunan to Kuling was a problem. It could take ten days each way, which rather took the edge off a holiday. The missionary community on the hill often arranged big evangelistic gatherings. I believe Billy Graham first found his vocation at Kuling.

Shaoyang

It was September 1920 before we were really in our own little home at Shaoyang, a small mud-brick bungalow erected a few years earlier. We had two bedrooms, dining room, study and Chinese kitchen. No running water. Bucket sanitation. Baths were wooden tubs made by the local cooper. Night soil was removed daily by farmers who even paid for the privilege to get valuable manure. This system of sanitation was universal and often complicated life and hospital arrangements during our years at Shaoyang.

House Servants

In those early days we were told that we would need to employ three servants: 'cook', 'boy', and 'amah'. Cook was the head-man. Besides preparing meals he had to go out every day to the street markets to get supplies. This was essential because otherwise we were

128

家遺先生惠存

弟陳光中敬贈 民國廿七年

于寶慶

Chen Kwang-Chung, coolie, bandit, war lord, shot by the
Reds at Shaoyang, 1951. Autographed portrait presented to
the Author, 1938

Written judgement by the People's Court at Shaoyang, 1949,
after the Author's trial

Shaoyang refugee hosts at the feast at Rennie's Mill

quite helpless. Only he knew where to find the things we needed. Usually shops or traders allowed him a small commission. The receipts they gave showed only the nominal price. In the big towns this commission squeeze might be large, but in Shaoyang we always felt that our servants had their losses as well as their profits. For instance, if he bought eggs there was never any charge for any that turned out to be 'out-of-date'. He only charged for the good ones.

Our first cook, old Huang, was reputed also to be a snake charmer. After a short time he retired and gave place to the 'boy', Lo-ssu-fu, who was our cook for the next twenty years. He served well and faithfully. The 'boy's' duties were cleaning, washing-up, keeping all oil-lamps in trim, and carrying from well or river all the water used in the house. He always hoped to become a cook someday. 'Amah' was the woman servant. She made beds, did the laundry and the baby sitting. There was no outside laundry available. The use of all this labour was essential if the missionary was to get any time for language study, teaching or medical work, for none of these services was laid on as in England.

In later years, when the use of servants became unfashionable under the Reds, we ceased to employ a 'boy', but then we had to buy water—by the bucket load from outside carriers.

Mary was always making friends. Any man or woman who came to work in our home soon became a real personal friend. Our last cook was Hsiung-usu-fu, who served all through the Communist occupation and despite all Red indoctrination. When we finally left he had to make a choice, either taking a Trade Union ticket and work in town, or returning to his country home and working his share of the land under Land Nationalisation. We never knew which he decided to do.

Amahs varied. The most memorable was Hu-Ma, an elderly strapping woman from the country, who was for many years the children's trusted friend and companion. Of her Mary writes: 'At first Hu-Ma could not understand anything that I did. She was a raw countrywoman with a stolid, hopeless expression. She had a loud voice, was not very tidy and had few clothes. In summertime that did not matter. Everything was strange to her, the children's food, their clothing and their habits. I had to be constantly watching and teaching and doing things for her.

'She is now completely changed. She has learned her work well. She can wash and iron as well as I myself, makes beds, changes the linen on the right day and manages the children well. Of course, I still do a great deal, because I want to. Perhaps more remarkable is the way she has learned to play with the children. She does not now mind if I find her prancing round the room with them. She fairly revels in Baby Andrew, and pride beams from every pore if he demands Kitty's toast instead of his proper baby food! We find it amusing to hear Kitty talking to her. She addresses a remark to me, and then turns to Hu-Ma and says the same in Chinese.

'Hu-Ma is not a Christian. She has not even heard "the teaching" before coming to us, but she is honest, hardworking and cheerful and will make a fine Christian woman. We have family prayers each morning, in Chinese and there are chapel services, but she cannot always get to these. I suppose I ought to help a bit, but I am shy. She is older than I am, and. . . No, there isn't any real reason. It is often easier to hang back than doing a bit of missionary work like that. It is easier to take the women's classes occasionally. I must try sometime. I have just started having Chinese lessons again—the first for eight months—I do neglect the hum-drum plodding. It is no wonder I am not ready for bigger work.'

Elsewhere she writes: 'Babies undoubtedly do as much missionary work as many a grown-up. The four children now in Shaoyang (two Stanfields and two of ours) are quite a part of the missionary staff. Perhaps one of the most potent factors in our work is our home life.'

Other friends of Mary's included the 'Biblewomen' or Women Evangelists who were on the church staff from time to time. She loved to make time to work with them. All our hospital matrons, from Katie Castle onwards, always felt that they could come and talk over matters with her. Not infrequently it ended in a quiet telling off for the Doctor, if he needed it, and all was happy again. Gertrude Hughes, the last of our matrons, who was with us all through the Communist days, was like a daughter to Mary. In fact she used to begin her letters to her 'Dear Mother Pearson'.

'Living Chinese'
Were we justified, whilst in China, in trying to keep up even a modified European standard of life? It was debatable.

The Chinese people have an innate capacity for living, crowded in a small space or on the slenderest of means. From Mary's first days in China it was always a trouble to her that with our modest missionary means we had 'enough' while so many Chinese around us had so much less. She just longed to share completely with them. Yet when we used to talk it over, it never seemed practical domestic economics. She continued nevertheless, to be worried about it and

130

brought it up again and again in our conversation, wishing we could do something about it.

In part, our problem was caused by the then ruling exchange rates, which placed such a premium on English money and so placed us in an unexpected position of 'power' when overseas. The mission in London thought it was providing very economical houses for its workers, but in China that sum allowed the construction of large, roomy manses, like a large, old vicarage at home. Most of these early houses had in them a so-called 'Chinese guest room', an old Chinese institution intended to honour visitors to the house. But in these buildings it often became a sort of outer sanctum, to which visitors might come by a separate door, what with their spitting and other disconcerting habits, local guests could not be admitted to living rooms with carpets and warm fires and clean food!

It was not until after 1930 that ideas of this sort began to fade. It was an event when we could find even one Chinese friend with whom we could defy these early conventions by asking him to share a meal in our home. From then on regular Christian fellowship across all racial barriers became a real and treasured experience.

When our new house at the hospital was built we used sun dried mud brick. It was far and away the cheapest house built by our Mission and was largely made possible by Mary's willingness to put up with less. It was a first attempt to bridge the gap and to be a house which could be used by either Chinese or European. It was not until we found ourselves under Communism, that living standards did really approximate and local people were spending as much on food as ourselves. This was a development for which Mary had longed, though the force and cruelty by which the Reds so often inaugurated it, distressed and disappointed her.

Her Children

Christine (or Kitty) was five months old when we reached China the other four were all born at Shaoyang. We were each time, able to have the help of a trained nurse (English or Chinese), but I had to take full medical responsibility myself. Mary was willing to put up with our primitive conditions and I had essential hospital equipment at hand if necessary. Once operation was needed. It was surely a triumph of love plus faith which brought her through so wonderfully.

Apart from the usual children's complaints, only Baby Eleanor was ever seriously ill. At eighteen months she had a very severe attack of Bacilliary Dysentery. She was so ill that at one time it

131

seemed we had lost her. She had saline infusions for we did not at that time have the drugs that are now available, and it left her with a weak digestion for some years.

Fire

One day Mary and I were having tea in the sitting room, the children having been left in the nursery for a few moments, down the corridor. It was just after Christmas. We suddenly heard Christine rushing out of the nursery and crying. Going along I found the nursery full of smoke and fire gaining a hold. I was able to open the window and tip burning clothes and furniture outside before the room itself caught fire. The open fire in the fireplace had been surrounded by wooden safety rails. Apparently Christine had been burning Christmas decorations and had set fire to drying clothes. It gave us all a fright. The baby was asleep in the next room all through it!

Praying About It

We returned home after our first seven years, with four strapping busy youngsters. They had grown strong running around or tumbling in the straw in the cow-house, and Christine had had one term at school in Kuling. This was 1927. The question now arose—what about schooling for the two older ones? The Kuling school had closed. We had no relatives able to take on their care. My father, then eighty, was too old to do much. What could we do? Stay in England and give up our China work; or had I to go back leaving Mary with the children in England? We just prayed, quite simply and repeatedly about it, and I asked the Mission Committee in London to join us in praying about the matter. Mary accepted it all as part of her privilege as a missionary wife and mother. Rev. A. W. Grist was at that time the China Secretary of the M.M.S. in London.

Shortly after this, Mr Grist received a letter from a single lady, saying that her parents had recently died and left her alone in a small country house. Did the Society possibly know of any missionary who had perhaps two little boys needing a home while their parents were away? Mr Grist took this as an answer to prayer. He did know of a boy and a girl needing just such a home. He enquired further about the writer and was eventually able to introduce us to Miss Marion Young, a Methodist Preacher's daughter, living at Arclid, Cheshire, not so far from our own district. We went over to see her and she soon became a much-loved 'Auntie Marion' to Christine and Andrew. Later on Eleanor and Philip shared her hospitality. During term time they were all together at Kingsmoor

School, Glossop. In years when we were both abroad, Arclid was their holiday home. We all owe a great debt to Miss Young, now Mrs Boffey.

Furlough Homes

Where to live whenever we returned home with our happy family, was always a problem for us. On our first furlough, the problem was solved for us when Mary's brother-in-law, Joe McLean, himself invested in a small 'semi' at Bidston Avenue, Birkenhead. On later furloughs we tried to rent, but in the end had to buy a house on a Building Society Mortgage, paying £900 for a house that had been built for £450. It was wartime and values were always increasing. After some years it sold for £1,750. But that was after we had held on to it, because Mary wanted to help a young married couple to have their own home while we were abroad. She often reminded me of her business acumen in that transaction, but she did it for love.

In 1943, while I was abroad, Mary had been compelled to evacuate our home with the family because of a bomb which fell at the end of their road in Wallasey. Somehow, travelling along bombed railways and disorganized towns, she was able to find a house to rent at Cheadle Hulme, and moved there after some hair-raising journeys through Manchester and Liverpool bombing raids. Perhaps this was one factor which brought on her severe depression in the months that followed. It was not until some time after my recall from the field that she was once again her happy self.

Depressions

As her family of children got into its teens, Mary began to have from time to time, periods of acute mental depression. During these seasons she always looked so sad and worried, and could hardly bear to take any responsibility or make any decisions. These sad times often lasted for months together. She usually just managed, with help, to carry on a daily routine. It left its mark on her. Even photographs taken at these times show at once how she was feeling.

She had the benefit of all the latest medical treatments, though never with much obvious immediate benefit. Each time after months or weeks she did eventually pull round and regain her normal control. Good friends certainly helped, not least Doctor Edith Hudgell of Harley Street, Rev. W. J. Hartley and others. Through the years she must have had quite half a dozen of these dreaded times.

In between came her good times, the times when she felt so well

133

and happy, and so full of life and sympathy. She then seemed to want to make up for all the times when she had been unable to do things.

Her Work at Shaoyang

When she was at Shaoyang, and well enough to do it, Mary always took a full part in the women's side of the church work. Often it was just helping with small meetings of almost uneducated women, trying to give them fresh ideas on how to look after their homes and children. On one occasion they got Mrs Wright to come and give her small baby a proper bath on the stage in front of all the mothers.

In 1948 she writes: 'Yesterday I had five different sorts of classes. 1. An English class for the middle Nursing class, ten of them. 2. A Chinese lesson for myself. 3. An English lesson for the Mission Primary school—20 boys and girls, ages 12 to 15. 4. An hour teaching a class of adult women at the Short-stay Women's school, at the chapel. 5. At 3 p.m. An English talk to 150 boys and girls of the Government 6th Middle School. After that I visited our German friends, the Gresse's, in the city and did a bit of baby-worshipping. Our Women's school is specially interesting. It is good to see the progress made by some of the pupils. One girl of sixteen, who knew nothing a year ago, is learning well. But there are also the "old dears" who come every year but can make nothing of it. Still, they hear the stories and enjoy the fellowship. One of them has such a nice smiley face, it is a treat to see her!'

About 1947, Mary took on a job of teaching a regular English class in one of the big Government middle schools in town, but found it an impossible task. Her senior class held over fifty boys of all ages, some men over twenty, whose previous learning of English had been appalling. She always had strict ideas of how things should be done, and this class almost broke her heart. Some of the boys had no intention of learning any English at all, but when it came to the exams and she failed them, there was consternation! They rolled up to try and get her to alter the marks. One big fellow was in tears: 'But I have to get married this week and if I have no pass I can't get married' was his plea. After that, Mary did not attempt further outside teaching. It was too much for her.

In the Nursing School she helped wherever she could, especially with the English classes, and often as a sort of mother-confessor to a lonely and perhaps, inexperienced, matron.

Family Weddings

Eleanor was married at home while we were in Hunan, so I have no first-hand details to record here.

Andrew's Wedding

It was November 1948, Andrew was already working in Hankow. His fiancée, Jean Frost, was travelling out with Frances, still a schoolgirl, who was to have a few months in Hunan with us. The wedding was to be in Hankow. A letter of Mary's dated January, 1949, tells the story:

'Andrew and I had gone to Hong Kong by train to meet the two girls. The great moment was when we spotted them on their boat at the quayside. All was excitement. We were soon introduced to various boat friends, including a young Scottish couple, the new Consul for Hankow and his wife.

'The next two days were a whirl of shopping, but by 1 p.m. on Wednesday we were all at the station in good time for the train for Canton. Our party included the new Consul. All was O.K. Having left Andrew passing the luggage through customs, I went off to visit the bank nearby. Judge my astonishment when I returned to the station and found it completely deserted! Was this just a bad dream? Enquiring where the train was I was told it had left five minutes ago! The time tables had been altered!

'On the advice of a friendly official, I quickly hurried to the office of British Airways, not far away, where I was most courteously treated by the manager, who went to a lot of trouble to get me a seat on a plane just due to start for Canton. I was not very big and had no luggage. I had just finished paying my fare when in walked Andrew! He had been in the post office next to the station when he looked up and found the train had gone, with all the newcomers including the bride and the Consul who could speak no Chinese. He too enquired, and found that a grey-haired lady was in the same plight, and that she had gone to the airways office . . . We could not have two seats, so he used my ticket and I would follow next day. I duly saw him off. He was actually in Canton before the train, and to the surprise of all, met them on the platform! I flew on the plane next day.

'The train journey north went well, we gradually donned more clothes as it got colder. Arrived at Wuchang, the Consular launch made crossing the Yangtse easy.

'The wedding was on November 30. Rev. J. J. Heady performed the ceremony very beautifully assisted by two Chinese ministers. The

135

hymns were chosen so that they could be sung in the two languages simultaneously. The service was held in the chapel of the Methodist Hospital, Hankow, where Andrew was already on the staff. The reception was at Doctor and Mrs Cundall's home. Jean wore a full skirted, long sleeved, white silk frock and a long veil, lent by Kit Gilliland. Doctor Peter Hsin was best man. After the reception came the reading of telegrams and speeches. George ended by saying that though the weather might be cold at the mountain at Kuling, (where they were going for a honeymoon) there would be no frost there! Frances and I are now back at Shaoyang and busy with lessons and we wonder what political developments are taking place around us.'

They might well wonder. The Communist armies were on their way!

CHAPTER FIFTEEN

More of Mary

Her Letters

WHAT a letter writer Mary was! She never allowed distance to become a barrier between herself and others. Postage stamps were the one thing in which she was quite prodigal—expense no object. She felt it to be so important to keep contacts. Letters made this possible. In everything else her wants were so few. She spent little on dress or personal things. In her home, food and even travel she was abstemious and economical almost to a fault. All account keeping bothered her, but she was determined to keep in touch with all her friends and loved ones.

At times, when I was abroad and she at home, she wrote regularly, never less than once a week. What a joy it was to get her letters. Yet very few of them have survived, partly of course, because of frequent hurried removals and also due to the fact of their very volume. I have been glad to find that a few of her letters to the children at school, 1946-50, still survive, and I am making what use I can of these.

Also, even with the letters which do survive, I do not find them easy to use for a purpose like my present one. They are not just factual accounts of 'things'. They are concerned with family happenings. What this child said. What had happened when they had returned to school. 'Had someone had a cold or cough?' She was so pleased that they had been able to visit her sister Elizabeth. 'I do hope you will get this in time for your birthday.' 'How does that new dress fit?' and so on.

And so the letters go on pouring out all the love of a mother's heart separated so far from her growing brood. What a wonderful mother she was!

One time in 1946 she quotes an old diary of her own from 1926: Kitty: 'You know, Andrew, Father Christmas is really Daddy and Mummy.' Andrew: 'Our best Mummy?' Kitty: 'No, just our Mummy who tells us what to do.'

After Frances had been out with us in 1948 and had to return to England because of the coming Red invasion, Mary took her by train to the boat at Hong Kong, whence she sailed with a missionary colleague. Mary writes: 'Being a mother, I can't put anxious thoughts away.' That was always the pull with her.

Or just occasionally she describes an unusual experience.

In 1947 she tells of a bus journey to Changsha from Shaoyang, 150 miles. She never found the 'rough and tumble' easy:—'We passengers

137

were all unbelievably crowded. Each one had only the tiniest wooden seat, wedged tight amongst other people and all their luggage. Road dust was thick in the air and into everything. This time the bus got a puncture, which meant a two hours' wait by the dry, dusty roadside. Then a few miles farther on the driver stopped to get himself a meal. There were still more delays crossing over the river at Siangtan. The road was very hard and bumpy all day and the 150 miles used up all the daylight of a long summer's day.'

When she did finally reach Changsha, all she could do was to lie flat on her bed and refuse all food until next day, in fact, she was quite sick. But next day she was as perky as ever.

At times too, Mary felt lonely at Shaoyang. On the day that Philip left us to go to England, travelling with the Stanfield family, she writes: 'Daddy had to go away on a country journey the day after Pip left. It seemed so strange to sit down to meals all by myself, especially at dinner time.' (The previous eight or nine days we had had Mr and Mrs E. Wright and Auntie Cuthie (Mrs C. V. Cook) to midday meals.) 'But I should not say that I sat down alone, because I had young Frances in her high chair close beside me. She looked so surprised when she saw only Mummy there—but as long as Mummy was there, she did not mind . . . One day it will be the day when we are all together again.'

Mary's Poems

It was during the last eighteen months of her life that Mary again started writing poetry. She had been stimulated to attempt it at a conference of 'Camps Farthest Out' (an evangelistic movement) at Swanwick. I only have space for a few quite memorable examples.

TOWARDS DAWN—HOUSEHOLD UNAWARE

The beauty of the morning sky
    Which I alone can see,
How can I tell the loveliness
    Or what it means to me?

The softest greys, bright pinks and blues
    And that ethereal green.
No words of mine can tell to you
    The wonders I have seen.

The beauty of the morning sky
    How fast it fades away
But I have stored it in my heart
    To last throughout the day.

138

SEPTEMBER THOUGHTS—BEFORE DAWN

(These lines describe the garden which she could see from her sick-bed at Chasetown)

The gleam of white dahlias in the dim morning light
Fore-shadowing all the colours that will soon meet the light.
The first sleepy twitt'rings of an early waking bird
With its promise of the full song that soon may be heard.
The distant hum of lorries on the busy Watling Street
Which stretches far to north and south till other great roads meet.
The blackbird's quick alarm note and the robin's tee-tee-tee,
And Orion coming up behind the sycamore tree.
Then robin into full song bursts and dunnocks sweetly sing.
Oh! The fresh'ning air, the sights and sounds, and God is Everything.

EYES TO SEE AND EARS TO HEAR

(More lines from Mary's sick-bed—September 1960)

The sight of one small flittermouse with quickly fluttering wings,
The blackbird's poignant melody as all alone he sings,
Sweet robin's tick-tick-ticking with a burst of song between,
So near he is to listen to, but never to be seen.

How can I pass it on to those who've never heard Thee speak?
Oh teach me how to do it for I am very weak.
Why! There's the great big golden sun, red-glowing mid the grey;
Is that the answer to my cry? What is it Thou would'st say?
The sun was still hidden by the little roof next door
Until I sat straight up in bed—then I could tell you more.
And now the sun's too bright for eyes that may not glory see.
'So bow your head and humbly pray, and truly worship Me.
'Then shall you learn the lessons, so many still to learn
'Then I can fill your heart with love until it glow and burn.
'But just remember to be kind to feeble Brother Ass,
'Remember all the stony roads through which he's had to pass.
'He's served you well and faithfully through nearly seventy years
'(Well, that's excepting one or two), through darknesses and fears,
'Through many joys and happiness, in lands both far and near.
'So treat him with respect and even cosset him, my dear.
'But still you'll find that there is many a work for you to do
'If only you obey me and love me well and true.'
Dear Lord, my heart I offer, I would Thy servant be
Please take me and employ me, and keep me close to Thee.

C.M.P.

Mary's Prayer Diary

For long years before her final illness, Mary had cultivated the habit of early rising. She maintained an uninterrupted time for prayer and quiet. She would be up by 6 a.m., or in later years when she was sometimes wakeful, it might be 5 a.m. when she turned out. She would then put on plenty of warm things, for comfort not appearance and seek out a quiet place, and turn on the light and the electric heater if there was one. With her Bible and her copy of Oldham's *Devotional Diary* in hand and writing materials available, she would sit down for her 'Quiet Time', her Morning Watch. A full hour would thus be passed until it was time to be getting the family breakfast. But first she would come back to our room and we would have our short time of prayer together, our regular custom before starting the day. She often used to chide me when I only barely managed to get ten minutes of quiet time myself before breakfast. Did I really think that was enough for such an important assignment?

Her copy of 'Oldham' is in my hands as I write this. It is a fairly new copy because her original one, which she had used and annotated for years, was confiscated by the Shaoyang Communist Police searching for spies and wireless! They could not understand what all these pencilled notes were. I hope they managed to understand it. She missed the confiscated book a lot, and as soon as we got home she bought a new one. Several blank pages in the book are filled with closely written notes of things and people to be prayed for. These were all in lead pencil and were regularly rubbed out and brought up to date as circumstances and people changed. It was thus never a static thing, but a live list of real needs for which she engaged herself to pray.

Years earlier (1936), when we had both learned much from the then Oxford Group (later M.R.A.), she got this habit of writing down any thoughts or guidance which might come during her praying time.

What were the things thus so dear to her heart? Under '*Daily*' come husband and children. Then a list of friends and neighbours in whom she had some special interest. Friends in China; her daily helper in the home and all the current political leaders of the world, Krustchev, Hammarskjöld, Mao, the Congo, the need for more missionary candidates. A whole page follows to the names of Chinese workers whom we had grown to love; 107 names in all are there, from hospital, church or schools in Shaoyang. And each day has another list of names centred round some special activity, like peace, youth work, re-union or healing.

It was during Mary's last eighteen months in England that it became apparent that, quite apart from her depressions her heart was not functioning as it used to do. She herself realized that she needed to go slow and to rest occasionally. In June 1960 therefore, she and I went for a never-to-be-forgotten holiday in Cornwall. We travelled by car and stayed at a small guest-house in Mullion kept by Miss Tripconey, a staunch local Methodist. Each day we would motor to one of the many viewpoints on the coast. Mary would take a short walk and then sit reading or sketching while I wandered farther afield. How she did enjoy all the wonder of it! Thus we visited and absorbed Mullion Cove, Coverack, Kynance Cove, Gunwalloe Sands, Lizard town and lifeboat station and other beauty spots. At Kynance, greatly daring, I allowed her to walk right down the steep path to the glorious sands. By going very slow and with help, she made the hard walk back without undue distress.

On our way home we stopped for a few hours at Clovelly, and I began to fear that we had got into trouble as the narrow village path took us down and down from the car park. Would she ever be able to walk back? At length she agreed to sit down on a view-point bench while I went to explore. What was my joy when right by the harbour at the bottom, I discovered a bus-stop sign, from which jeeps were chair-lifting visitors back to the top. And so she was able to enjoy the whole of the walk right down to the sea, after all. I was indeed thankful.

When we had started this holiday she was still in one of her depressed moods, but during these lovely, restful days, I could feel the depression gradually lifting each day. It was an extraordinary experience to be with her and to feel how each day she was becoming more able to appreciate and to enjoy, and to respond to life. It was on the long drive home as we got into the Black Country, and when our car was being very difficult because of clutch trouble, that she suddenly said to me: 'George, I'm all right now. I can do things again.' And she was! She was once again her full, normal self, and as before she wanted to be doing everything at once.

Two weeks later however, her heart began to rebel at such treatment. She had to take to bed and rest again. But she never again had any more depression.

In October she insisted on going on holiday to Scotland. I protested. She wanted to go by car and to call on all her friends everywhere on the way. I suggested train, as I thought that would be straight there and back. So train it was. We primarily went to stay with her friends the Connellys at Inellan near Dunoon, but she must also visit her sister Phyllis at Haltwhistle. Having arrived in Scotland she would not be held in. She insisted on crossing Scotland to visit relatives in Edinburgh, and back, all by herself, and a steamer trip to Tighnabruich, bringing back old childhood memories of fifty years ago. How she did enjoy it all! But the return journey to England was a broken and difficult one. No through train, and platform bridges which were a menace to her poor heart. I was indeed glad when we were once more at home. Then it had to be bed and more times in and out of hospital, under the loving care of Doctor Clifford Parsons.

I was still busy with the daily chores of General Practice. 'You've gone on too long,' she said reproachfully, one day. I was then already busy getting a small bungalow built for us to retire to. But it was not to be.

Her Springtime

I think it was on February 9, 1961, that I had been out on my morning rounds, leaving Mary in bed and Mrs Rigby, her loved helper, on duty at the house. When I got back Mrs Rigby was very worried. Mary had got out of bed by herself and had fallen. Mrs Rigby had got her back into bed, but Mary could not speak. It was her fateful stroke, due to thrombosis and clots from her failing heart. Mary never spoke again but she soon understood all that was said to her and responding with nods of 'yes' or 'no'. Nursing now became a major difficulty, so it was hospital again, and her last few days were spent in Ward Two of Birmingham General Hospital, where Sister Scattergood and a German Staff Nurse were kindness itself to her. They found her such a grateful patient to nurse. She gradually learned in those days to hiss a sort of 'yes' as well as to nod in response to questions.

One afternoon, sitting beside her, I read to her some of our wonderful old Christian hymns, and especially Baxter's:

> My knowledge of that life is small,
>   The eye of faith is dim,
> But 'tis enough that Christ knows all
>   And I shall be with Him.

As I finished reading and stopped, she suddenly whispered such an emphatic 'Yes, yes, yes'. Those were her last words. A day or so later, on a Sunday morning, February 19, 1961, Sister Scattergood called for me on the telephone. I went over at once with Frances. I took Mary a few spring snowdrops and crocuses from our own garden. She looked up as we came in and smiled, too feeble for speech, and while we were out of the room for a few minutes for the nurses to attend to her, she was gone. Minutes later, Christine and Sister Elizabeth were also with us.

Yes, February 19, 1961, was truly her springtime, her new beginning. She had gone to be with Him, and she has left us too with that great hope that we may be worthy to follow after.

What a wife I had—nay—still have.

Her funeral was on February 24th. That evening, after I had been busy taking departing guests to their trains, I was returning home in my car, when suddenly the setting sun broke through the low grey cloud with an unforgettable red glow . . . to welcome her home?

Yes, this is all true but I do not want to give the impression that we ever attained a complete romantic one-ness of our personalities. We were always two very different people and from time to time this used to worry Mary. We often saw a situation differently. Occasionally we even almost quarrelled. That hurt both of us; but then we prayed about it, together, and . . . well, we were soon all smiles again, and life together continued as such a wonderful adventure.

CHAPTER SIXTEEN

Liberation, 1949

HAVING spoken in our last chapter of 1961 events, we now go back in time to look at events in 1949.

The Empty Days. Living in a Vacuum

Early on in 1949 it became evident that Chiang-Kai-shek and the Kuomingtang Government were fighting a losing battle against the Red Armies, which were slowly easing their way south and into Hunan. Mary and I were together in Shaoyang at this time, and also Gertrude Hughes as Matron. We believed that it might be possible for us to stay on and continue hospital work.

Meanwhile the currency situation got worse and worse. 'When would they come?' was the question in everyone's mind. The old local government was every day getting more and more futile, and more and more corrupt. The official paper currency was becoming virtually unusable and the only money that would buy anything was the ancient solid silver—if you could find it.

Perhaps quotations from a few letters written during those days will paint the situation more vividly:

April 1949. All authority in this area seems to have vanished. A few folk in the Magistrate's office are still there to be looked at. So many fixed points are dissolving. Already a large area in our circuit is definitely under (hidden) Red civilian control. This has established itself, made its peace with the old-style provincial authority, and is already proceeding unopposed to deprive land-owners of land and grain, leaving them enough for personal use only. The result at present is that nobody dare work the land. It just goes out of cultivation.

'At the same time the old army is still active, its press-gang busy conscripting poor little farmer boys as soldiers. One sergeant was heard to say: "Let's go to So-and-so village. The farmers are not expecting us and we'll get plenty of boys." And then they look after them worse than if they were dealing with sheep or cattle. Last week a party of four such recruiting sergeants and their new recruits were billeted in a farmhouse. Overnight the sergeants themselves dug a hole through the mud-brick wall and decamped—to join the Red Army, leaving their recruits free.'

A little earlier in May 1947, an incident occurred in Shaoyang which opened a small window into the political underworld. I wrote: 'There has been a big political row in town this week. I was called out to give first-aid to two men from a shop in the city which had just been burned out. The condition of the men was unusual. In the end it turned out they were assistants at the shop, a goldsmith's, and that they had been drugged before the fire. The "Number Two" official under the City Magistrate had been round one night and had compelled all the assistants to swallow twenty tablets of veronal. While they all slept he robbed the shop, and then set it on fire. One of the assistants lost his life. Now it is has all come to light. The stolen goods have been recovered and it has become a nation-wide sensation. All the Chinese papers are full of it. A suggestion was made that the veronal had come from our hospital, but this was disproved, I guess there will be a shake-up of local officials.

'Hospital work keeps me busy. We now have a third Chinese doctor on our staff.'

July 1949 'Here nothing much happens. The expected "Red Liberation" seems farther off than ever. Every possible building in town is occupied by soldiers of every description, of Chiang-Kai-shek's army. None of them has been paid over the past four months, so that they want everything free from the populace. People say there have been two disasters this summer. First the "Water disaster" (the flood) and now the "Soldier disaster". The same miserable defenders make up quite fifty per cent of our daily clinics. They want all for nothing. The wretched authorities pay not a penny; the whole show is bankrupt. Only silver dollars will buy anything. Once again we are learning to sound or "ring" every dollar to see if its silver is true. Even old Austrian thalers of Maria Theresa, dated 1798, have come into circulation.' (Later I heard that these thalers were really new and had been minted at the London mint!)

'Local officials are almost starving. No proper tax collection is possible. "White" refugees from down river are coming into town, wearing their finest silk clothing and red toenails (the only red thing that they do like). Our Methodist Chairman, Rev. Chang Mou-shang from Changsha, has been visiting us. His advice to us is "Stay put. Carry on". There are likely to be hard times for the church, but churches in the north are even now carrying on under the new conditions. It is great to have such a man in charge these days.'

And in August 1949, I wrote: 'In hospital we are getting less normal work for people dare not travel, but this is compensated for by war wounded from recent bombing raids. It is a curious feeling waiting here. If not already isolated from the world, we are likely soon to be so. We do not know whether mission monies will be able to come through to us or whether we may be entirely dependent on

145

local hospital income. Ministers and preachers cannot foresee how they can live in the future. Some will certainly have to look for outside work, but will continue preaching. We are going forward into a vacuum, living by faith from day to day. Keep on praying for us all even when letters are few and far between. And keep writing. One never knows when a letter may get through. How go your own affairs? . . .'

The Red Army Arrives. 'Liberation'

It was on October 6th, 1949, that the Red Revolution really caught up with us and a change occurred which profoundly affected every aspect of our life and work in Shaoyang. We had been 'liberated'.

For weeks beforehand we had been getting reports of the rapid advance of the Red Armies from North China, through Hankow, then into Northern Hunan, then Changsha, always nearer to us. The next day many wounded Red soldiers were brought into town and simply dumped in the streets. Chiang's men had no more time for such.

We at once got permission to do what we could for them. I and some of our nurses went along the rows of helpless men in the streets with a few stretcher-bearers. We selected just the worst cases and moved them into our wards until all beds were full. The rest might attend as out-patients. Fighting continued for some days, but Chiang was fighting his losing battle. On October 5th leaflets from Communist sources were distributed throughout the town: '*From the People's Liberation Army to the People of Shaoyang.* We have won the battle. Tomorrow our forces will enter Shaoyang. We come to liberate and protect you all. Come out on to the road tomorrow midday and welcome us to Shaoyang.'

Next day, about noon, I joined the big crowds round the bus station and along the motor road. Red Flags were everywhere. Where only yesterday Kuomingtang flags had flown, not one was left, and the last Kuomingtang soldier or official had disappeared. After a long hot wait we at last saw vehicles coming slowly down the long straight road. As they got closer we saw that in front of all was a group of girls in costume, on foot, dancing and singing what we were soon to learn as the new Chinese National Anthem.

Following the girls were lorries full of China's youth, boys and girls from middle schools and colleges, all dressed in rough soldiers' uniform and armed. These, we soon found, were to be the spearhead of the new civilian government. They had been attracted into the new regime, given a month or two of special instruction, and were now being sent to their new jobs. Some were 'propaganda corps', others were to be the new 'Civil Service'. All were sent out amongst the common people to tell them the good news of 'liberation from economic fear'.

The lorries were all camouflaged with nets and tree branches, for there had been bombing the day before. Behind the lorries came the big guns and armament, all of them American! Captured a day or two earlier from Chiang's retreating troops. And so they entered our city as conquerors. The Kuomingtang never made another real stand. Their men scattered in all directions or came at the first opportunity to join the victors.

The Two Armies

For long we had known the K.M.T. of Chiang Kai-shek troops in our area as a disorganized rabble, badly clothed, ill fed and diseased. They had no proper medical service. If a man fell ill he gave up his rifle and was left by the roadside to fend for himself. We often got such men at hospital. The officers were hopelessly corrupt and got rich by indenting for supplies for more men than they had, and by starving them too. Discipline was mostly non-existent. (Was not the English army in the days of Good Queen Bess in a very similar condition?)

The Red Army which entered Shaoyang was a great contrast; to us a new experience. Officers and men appeared to be dressed alike, all in good warm, winter uniforms. There was strict discipline. All fed alike. The men knew what they were doing and why. Daily cell meetings were held at which officers and other ranks mixed and asked, and answered questions. Each one felt that he was a part of a great organized movement. Each had his or her part to play. Yes, we found that some of their soldiers were women, all under the same strict discipline and with a strict puritanical behaviour and a great enthusiasm for their cause. Officers, though not distinguished by any uniform, were well known and obeyed.

The New Government Gets to Work

After the arrival of the Red Army we soon began to see changes. We found that we now had a financially honest Government, where 'yes' meant 'yes' and 'no 'meant 'no'. But every word, every action, had to be certified by two officials, both equally responsible, with their lives if necessary, *and* to be approved by committee. All the old corruption was swept away overnight.

Very soon they were on our trail as foreigners. They began a close check-up on all we were doing, and were obviously pleased when

147

they found their own wounded men being so happily cared for in our wards. The propaganda squads were everywhere. Comrades would come round and sit down for hours just talking to our coolies as they worked or to the nurses in their Nurses Home, 'encouraging the nurses'. Everywhere the phrase was repeated: 'You have now been liberated. You must change your way of thinking. You must no longer work to get rich. You will work because you love your country and your people and it is your duty to serve them.'

To all of which the common people replied: 'Don't be silly. How can a man change the way he thinks?'

But the propagandists continued, over, and over, and over again, in the same words. Big meetings were called at all times of day or night, at which the attendance of all coolies, nurses and staff was compulsory, when the new thinking was expounded over and over again. Then criticism was asked for, and when made from the floor of the meeting, was replied to by again asserting the 'correct line', again and again, and on and on, until the tired listeners at last had no more to say, and the meeting closed after a declaration that it was unanimously in favour of the party line.

All this took a lot of time. Not everyone understood everything at once, but the underdog was always encouraged to protest. One day a peasant was growling to a soldier about some new regulations not to his taste. 'What's the matter,' replied the soldier, 'you've been liberated, what more do you want?'

'Poor peasants' and 'working coolies' were constantly being urged to 'Stand up and speak up'. To say out what they were feeling, and to denounce their oppressors if they had any grudges against those formerly in power. This led to a lot of unhappiness and tragedy, including murders and suicides of those who felt that all society had collapsed and that there was no way out! Incidentally, I know of no suicides amongst our Christian members.

When one asked whether there had not been some good landlords in the old days, always came the reply: 'No, there are no good landlords. All landlords must be liquidated. They are all anti-social because they have been living off land which they did not work themselves. It is not allowed to love them nor to give them any help.' This, of course, was nothing but persecution and led to untold misery among many decent folk whose only crime was that they had been born in a certain family.

Local prisons were soon full of the New Poor, to whom we as church workers no longer had an entry. I saw a very tragic column of

148

these prisoners one day, being led bound through the streets, dressed now in only the very poorest of clothes.

Taxes

Very heavy taxation was soon instituted, and also 'compulsory loans' from any who had money. To be 'with it' I also made a small loan. All rice stores were checked and a requisition was made, leaving only a fixed weight of rice for each individual's food. We were soon hearing complaints that this did not leave enough food to carry through till next harvest in July-August. In towns a 'business turn-over tax' appeared and a stamp tax on all receipts. All this was not what the revolutionaries had expected, but it was all part of the campaign to rehabilitate national finances and to stop the runaway inflation. In this it was successful. At first, churches were taxed, but this was rescinded later.

Cells

Looking back on these months of 'liberation' the heart of much of the reforms does seem to have been in the 'Cells' or Small Groups. Organization of these began quite soon after the arrival of the Red Army. Each cell meeting contained about twelve to twenty people from the near neighbourhood. They had to meet many times each week and everyone must be in a 'cell'. Their first task was to read through and discuss in detail the writings of Mao-Tse-tung and the other leaders.

Each cell had its Leader and its Deputy Leader who were jointly responsible for the correct thinking and opinions of each of their members and reforming the thought of any who did not conform. I myself attended some of the early cell meetings in hospital, but I did not continue. It seemed pointless to me at the time. I found Mao's new phraseology difficult to understand, and the constantly desired confessions of past sins committed against society, I found often forced and at times apt to be said with tongue in cheek. I must add that later it seemed as though people did begin to believe what they so constantly repeated.

Anyway, regulations were not applied to me as I was a foreigner who had already asked for his return visa to England. Again and again I found that these meetings might have been modelled on an early Methodist class meeting, with its responsible Leader or Lay pastor, and with the mutual care and interest of all in the progress of each member.

From time to time new subjects or campaigns were sent down,

started from Peking, which everyone must learn about, discuss and approve! Such were 'Oppose America', 'Help Korea', 'Land reform' in all its aspects or 'the three Antis' (San Fan), (the eradication of Corruption, Waste and Dictatorship) etc. etc. It has been suggested that the oversight and care of these cells for their members became almost a substitute for the old clan organization. This was probably true, for the Chinese people well know how to live together at very close quarters, and they enjoy being in a crowd. They are used to it and do not mind learning to think alike. They thus do not feel that their freedom is being infringed by these methods.

Red Success

However good the organization there must surely have been some measure of mass hysteria or hypnotism present, for the way in which all these new ideas were accepted by the bulk of the people was astounding. It accomplished changes in life and thought and ways of living which any ordinary citizen speaking in advance, would have said were quite impossible. People's thoughts did change. They became new people, honest, clean and keen to serve their country and society! Formerly suppressed and down-trodden coolies and workers gradually became intelligent leaders.

Some of our younger nurses and coolies were carried away by the new enthusiasms. To them it seemed as though the Kingdom of Heaven had arrived in Shaoyang, a New Utopia in which they could share. A number of our girls left their hospital work to go into the new propaganda Corps for whole-time work.

Soon we began to hear a new slogan: 'Produce. Produce. Produce'. Everyone must produce all the food he could. Our nurses began to dig up bits of garden and plant cabbages to the neglect of ward work—until the organizers came round and saw what was happening. They then told the nurses that the best contribution to the production drive was to do their own job properly. Hospital work thereafter improved considerably.

Equality

There was no demand for the equalization of wages, but the poorest all got a substantial rise, to make which possible, in hospital, the senior staff asked that they might have, at the same time, a token reduction! The principle was maintained that higher qualifications get higher pay.

Coolies

Through this time it was often a real thrill to see our own hospital coolies blossom into live individuals, no longer afraid of dismissal or of 'the boss'. Although we had in the old days always tried to pay wages a little above the local minimum, with the increases given our coolies now had enough to get an occasional new cotton suit and to support their families, or even time to play organized games, like Basket Ball, with proper rules and an umpire. They had become human beings able to enjoy themselves.

I have a vote

In town, every worker, including myself, had to join his own Trade Union and pay his membership fee. Mine was the 'Union of Hospital Workers'. To me this did not mean much, except that when the first General Election came along, I found that I, a mere Englishman, had a vote at the election! There was some talk about a choice of candidates, but as I was not then meeting in a cell I knew little about them, and in the event I did not use my vote.

Senior Staff

The senior hospital staff were affected variously. Of course they too had to attend all the meetings, cells, etc. They had to survive criticism and counter-criticism, and to submit to constant interference with their own jobs by comrades who often knew little of what was needed. Hospital Business Manager, Wang Tu-tsai, an ex-schoolmaster with a long record of faithful work in his church, was in despair, and I think he only carried on in name, ceasing to have any real control. Doctor Huang was elected by his fellow-workers to follow me as Medical Superintendent, but I believe that he came under special scrutiny because he had been for a time in England for a post-graduate course of study, and he was later sent for prolonged courses of re-education, but it is good to know that he retained his job as Superintendent.

Before we left, Mr Fen, the then Hospital Evangelist, was elected as Assistant Superintendent, but he had a bad time. I think that they just could not understand why he had been promoted; he was repeatedly sent for by party or police. Towards the end of our time he came to look like a frightened rabbit. He was then quite afraid to speak to me at all, although some weeks earlier, when it first became known that Mary and I would be leaving, he had been the first to present us with a beautiful, illuminated scroll conveying his own

151

thanks and good wishes. I still prize this greatly, for he was surely a brave and persecuted Christian.

Only one among our trained staff became in any way antagonistic. This was the X-ray technician, Shih Chin-fa, a young boy who had just come back from a special training course. He went out of his way to make things difficult for us. One of our X-ray machines had broken down and could not be repaired. I had therefore, sent its essential parts to the maker's agent in Hong Kong for repair, but they could neither repair it there nor return it to Hunan, due to the break-down in communications. Shih went to the police and insisted that before Mary and I left, I must pay the hospital the full price of the machine, because I had given it away to the 'Imperialists'. This quite regardless of the fact that I myself had collected the money for the machine in England and presented it to the hospital. 'Excuses' did not concern him, poor boy, and I had to pay up.

When we did eventually reach Hong Kong, I was able to reclaim the still unrepaired machine and take it back to the Missionary Society in London. They got it put right and it was sent for use in a mission hospital elsewhere.

Letters

Letters written during these days make further interesting comments. On November 6th, 1949, one month after Liberation, I wrote: 'Today has surely been one of the greatest days in the history of the Shaoyang church. We have been having a visit from our Chairman, Rev. Chang Mou-sheng. He baptized twenty adults and six children. Afterwards there were ninety-eight church members present for Communion, such a crowd that they knelt right through the kneeling board at the Communion rail. Alas, it had dry rot—we were not used to such crowds. Some of the adults were nurses from hospital. The town now seems comfortably at peace. The soldiers of the Liberation Army are the best fed, the best looked after, and the most orderly we have seen for years, but they have a fully worked out scheme of 'Social Engineering' to change the face of the society that we have lived in so long.'

December 19th 1949

'Following the wage increases, hospital funds are now very tight. We can hardly make ends meet these days, but one of the first suggestions from the coolies' cell meeting was some ideas for saving on our coal consumption. That looks like co-operation. Investigations of all our work continue. Nothing is taken for granted. All my past accounts are being ransacked. Every time we meet there is a comrade onlooker, even in my Bible class. More and more they spread their 'good news' and new doctrines. Land re-distribution is promised soon. How many 'Vicars of Bray' are jumping onto the band-wagon I find it hard to say, but I have heard of some strange move-overs.

'We have been interested to meet numerous instances of Christians inside the Red Army ranks. One is a theological student who regularly keeps up his church going. Another, a medical officer, attended my Bible class last week and was a most helpful member of it. Nevertheless, the whole tendency is towards a materialism on the Russian model. There is 'Freedom of Religion' and 'Freedom to oppose Religion'—and sometimes the latter freedom is more free than the former. But materialistic thought is nothing new in China.'

February 26, 1950

Dear Philip,

'. . . It is the Chinese New Year. They now call it Spring Festival. This year every institution was instructed to get up a dancing team and to exchange entertainments with each other. The Communists have brought with them from North China the Yang-Ko Drum Dance. Using a coloured costume and silk shawls you walk along with a small hip-drum making a regular beat.

The rhythm is repeated *ad lib* in an almost hypnotic manner. It is a tremendous craze, arms at right-angles, shoulders loose, round and round they go by the hour. Sometimes you hear a slightly varied rhythm. Often there are words sung in praise of Mao Tse tung and the revolution.

'In hospital much of the former spick and span is missing. The Nursing Students Society Small Groups discuss everything and then they issue orders and appoint departmental heads from amongst themselves. Formerly they were treated largely as children, but the new system has thrown responsibility on them and to this they have reacted well. Recently one member of the senior class of nurses started staying out at nights and playing around. The students themselves called her to book, reported the matter and agreed that she be asked to leave, for she was letting Society down. For Miss Hughes, our Matron, discipline hardly exists at all in its old form. But ward work still goes on and duty hours are kept despite all distractions.'

153

Amid it all one of our senior nurse graduates, married but still on the staff, had a difficult confinement losing her baby and almost her life too. During her worst time several of our Christian women, led by our Amah, Mrs Chu nai-nai, spent a whole night in prayer for her, taking turns to keep awake.

CHAPTER SEVENTEEN

Revolution in Village and Countryside

SO FAR my story has been mostly about how I saw the Revolution from inside our hospital. This is inevitable, because during all these months I was continuously at work on the hospital premises, all day, every day. I had no opportunity to get out into the country round about. Even if I had wanted to go the new authorities would not have allowed an 'imperialist foreigner' to wander in the disturbed conditions then prevailing. My account therefore, of outside events must be one of hearsay. But I heard a lot.

New enthusiasts soon got to work in the villages. They held innumerable meetings urging the peasants to rebel against the local landlords and money-lenders, to get their own back on the 'oppressors'. Before long people in the villages were told to divide themselves into three classes. These were 'poor peasants', 'middle peasants' and 'rich peasants'. The poor peasants were those who owned no land and worked for other people. The middle ones were those owning just a little land, who worked their land without any hired labour. The rich peasants were those who owned more land than they could till and worked it with hired labour. Those classified as 'poor peasants' now found themselves to be the new aristocracy. They had priority at the Law Courts and everywhere, and could do no wrong. The 'middle peasants' were just tolerated. Those classified as 'rich' soon found that they were being put to all sorts of difficulties and disadvantages and were being rapidly reduced to the general level.

The rest, the few people not reckoned as 'peasants' at all, were the 'landlords' who owned much land. They were blamed and persecuted from every side, and could get no redress. Peasants were encouraged to pay back old injuries, real or imagined, and to demand immediate redress. Big village processions were organized to go 'en masse' to the richer homes and literally to 'hunt out the rich dogs'· I happened one day to see one of these peasant marches on its way to a landlord's home, armed with pick-axes and pitchforks to do its fell work. When found, these victims were often unceremoniously thrown out into the street, if not killed outright, and their houses were occupied by the 'poor peasants', or possibly the former owner would still be allowed one room in his own house. Even then the victims were watched all day long and every meal they ate was scrutinized to see if they kept back any hidden stores. They were soon starving. Is it surprising that some of the more energetic amongst them tried to form 'White underground' terror groups, and that both sides went about in fear from day to day?

More systematic land reform came a little later. It was highly organized according to a long laid plan. Special 'cadres' (officials) were trained and sent out to implement it. Every person, man, woman or child willing and able to work on the land was given his individual share of land. For a peasant with a large family this was quite adequate. He was provided with freehold title deeds. Agricultural instruments and plough animals were likewise distributed, though some had to share when there was not enough for everyone. Some of the former rich peasants and landlords took their share, many others just ran from home (or committed suicide), and were shot if caught.

Military officers of the old army who had not at once re-enlisted in the Red Army were shot at sight. Thousands must have perished in this mass murder. At one period, our cook, Chung Ssu-fu, used to come in each morning with the news that 'so many more were shot yesterday'. It was a time of fear and terror.

Open-air mass meetings were summoned (I was at the start of one such) where officials of the old regime were put on trial (so-called) prior to being shot; flags flying, bunting out everywhere and dancers to entertain the crowd. In all this it was obvious that the 'poor peasants', the great majority of the people, had much to gain, and the revolutionary regime could truly claim that they had the approval of the large majority for their doings.

The development of the large 'Producers Co-ops' and of the 'Peoples Communes' did not take place until long after we left in August 1951.

One of China's War-Lords

Working as I did, in one of the far corners of the country, I rarely or never, met the people who were making world head-lines. One 'War-Lord' however, I did get to know. This was General Chen 'Kwang-chung. His old home was the little village of Ku-Lou-Ting, only fifty yards from our front gate. Born in a coolie family he was given the baby name of 'San-Sheng', number three. Later he was 'Kwei-sheng', his school name. When we arrived he was among the small boys playing around our gate. As a young man he carried coolie loads in and out of of the city, and was well known to all our hospital coolies.

There came a day after the flood of 1924 when the main city bridge had been washed away, that a temporary bridge of boats had

156

been erected and a small toll was levied on passers by for the construction of the bridge.

Chen had to take his load across the bridge but he had no cash to pay the toll. What could he do? He just pushed the toll collector into the water and passed over. After that he was 'on the run'. The Yamen police were after him. With a few like-minded friends he went off into the countryside and got hold of a few guns. Together they began to raid unsuspecting rich homes, and to open their granaries. They next offered to sell the rice to all comers at half-price. Chen got the money, the local peasants got cheap food, so both were satisfied, and the rich man did not dare to complain to headquarters. It was a real case of Robin Hood over again.

This game continued for years, the band growing in strength and the goverment at its wits end to try to establish order. It ended when Chiang-Kai-shek's government offered Chen a commission in the army, on condition that he came in with all his men, who would become regular soldiers recognizing Chen as their commander. The plan worked and the countryside had peace again. Chen now took the name Kwang-chung, 'Light-of-the-Middle-Kingdom'. He had ambitions.

A few years later came the abortive first Communist attempt to take over Shaoyang. Word was passed to Chen who was by then in a far corner of Hunan. Without waiting for orders he marched his army right across the province and arrived at Shaoyang a few hours before the *coup* was due. The Red organizers (one of whom was a patient of ours, a teacher named Hsiang) were caught and killed. Again the countryside was quiet, and the Establishment was duly grateful. Chen Kwang-chung was a name with which to conjure.

Chen and his army remained in Shaoyang. In those days Shaoyang was on one of the main routes by which opium grown in the hills of the far west of China used to travel into China proper. He found that all he needed to do was to take a substantial tax on each load of opium. Opium was valuable stuff and he was soon fabulously rich, the owner of a goldmine!

As one means of investing his new gains he bought a large plot of land next door to the hospital. He would build a great clan home, the marvel of all comers. He used no architect, but wanted it to be 'modern' so he used to bring his builder along to my house and instruct him: 'I want one like this—or this.' Presently we would see some impossibly altered version going up. He would build one day and if he did not like the results he would pull it down the next and start something quite different, like a child playing with bricks.

157

During this period his eldest daughter fell ill with typhoid and was brought to hospital. I had to explain to him the necessity of prolonged care and skilful nursing. He, himself, understood what I said, for he was a highly intelligent, if uneducated. But his senior wife absolutely refused to allow the girl to stay in our wards. I argued, I pleaded, without effect. Back home she had to go. Again I spoke to Chen of the folly of thus treating such a serious case. 'Yes, I agree,' he said, 'but what can I do with these women? It is they who decide.' And that was that. The girl went home and died a few days later. He was thus quite helpless among the ignorant folk of his own clan.

After a time Chiang-Kai-shek moved Chen and his army to garrison duty in East China, perhaps an attempt to curb the Shaoyang opium trade. When the Japanese began to make trouble in the east, Chen's men had no desire to fight, nor any organized ability. At this point I do not know the whole story, but later we heard that Chen had been demoted and imprisoned by Chiang in Hankow.

He languished in prison for some time, but was released and returned to Shaoyang, a sadder but not wiser man. Once again he started to build—and to pull down what he had built. Money no object. He was by now marked down as an 'arch-enemy of the People' by the Reds.

When the Communist troops did take over Shaoyang in 1949, he was a much-wanted man. His big home was nationalized as a 'People's Hospital'. He was again on the run.

Suddenly one day he appeared alone at our hospital and demanded to see me at once. I met him. It was a risk even to speak to such a wanted man in those Communist days. What a change there was in him! There he sat on a stone seat half-way between the hospital and my house. A pathetic figure, worn out, swollen with dropsy, feeble in the extreme, obviously a dying man. 'Could I protect him or cure him?' was his plea. There was just nothing that I could do. Even to put him to bed in our wards would have been to invite his immediate arrest and execution. So he quietly left and we saw him no more. A few days later he was recognized by Communist peasants and handed over. After one of the great 'Popular Trials' he was shot out of hand.

And so ends a strange life story. I still have a portrait of him presented to me in the days of his great prosperity, in full uniform, medals and everything.

Schools and Early Red Contro

'The party' was always keen on getting schooling for everyone. Miss

158

Wen-I-fang, our deaconess, was most enthusiastic about this, and was trying to use their methods for the women she wanted to help. The Mission Primary School at Shaoyang had a long history of service, although in recent years it had been overshadowed by costly Government development of new schools. We were already using the full government curriculum and when the Reds came the school was told just to 'switch text-books' and carry on.

Soon the new authorities got busy calling for night schools for adults, classes for women, etc. As there were no other teachers available the Primary School teachers were expected to take these extra classes on a voluntary basis. They found themselves with three consecutive school populations on the same inadequate premises. The Primary children attended each morning, the women at 3 p.m. and at 6 p.m. the illiterate workers from the city were hauled in, and the poor teachers had to start all over again for the third time in one day. Loyally they tried to comply, but as the Headmaster Mr Li Chou said to me: 'We can't get time off even to eat a meal.' How long this system was able to continue I do not know. It could not last long for Mr Li Chou himself was known to me as a recent case of lung tuberculosis. He could not stand that strain for long.

This was perhaps typical of much of the early unregulated enthusiasm, with a quite thoughtless waste of resources and manpower, which we saw at the start. We did not see the end of it.

CHAPTER EIGHTEEN

Revolution in Hospital

Our Contacts with the New Officials

ONE THING that we soon noted in all officials of the new Government was a studied lack of the old common courtesies of life; the old mutual bow as a guest is leaving, the little polite word, or the polished pleasant conventional phrase, or the exaggerated reference to one's own unworthiness or to the other person's honour and attainments. All this suddenly had no place in the new world. It was all 'Yes', 'No' or 'Come', or 'I am going', not even a goodbye or its equivalent. After thirty years in China I felt something lacking.

The Free Treatment Question

A curious development of Communist rule was the way in which they repeatedly objected to the free treatment given to our poor patients in need. I have already recorded how they ordered us to stop giving any medical help to wounded from Chiang-Kai-shek's old army. Later they instructed me to cease all free treatment at our O.P.D. We must charge for all treatments, they said, because everyone in the new society had money to pay. (We however, still knew of many in need who could not possibly pay.) Did they feel that we were trying to steal the people's hearts from them?

At that stage almost all our free cases were people who had been sent to us by the Communist village Head man, who provided them with a travel pass and a letter of recommendation. I explained this to the official in charge. 'That of course, is O.K.,' he replied. 'Keep the records of all such cases and send them to my office each month.' At the end of the month I personally took the full list with all certificates attached, a goodly bundle, to the Police Office. I shall always remember how the officer on duty looked through that list and found a proper village certificate attached in every case. He got more and more disgusted. 'Take this away, it is in order,' he said. And so we continued Christian charity even in revolutionary China.

The Drugs Affair

It was early in 1950 that the Shaoyang Communist Medical Authorities paid me an official visit and asked to see all invoices of drugs purchased or presented to the hospital in the past few years. That was a tall order, for we had since VJ Day received a lot of drugs, etc. which were literally dumped on us from departing ex-U.S. Army Stores, Red Cross, etc. Most of them came without documentation of any sort. All had been unpacked and some had been used, for in those days it was almost impossible to buy medical stores at any price. We were now suspected of personal profiteering!

Owing to recent bombing raids I had got the stuff in half-a-dozen different store rooms. I therefore suggested that I show my questioners round and let them see what we still had, and how it was being cared for and used. They came round with me and what they saw they approved. They therefore said that they themselves would make a full invoice of everything and that that would be the list for which I was responsible. Accusations of profit-making would be waived.

Next day they sent round a team of dispensers who could read English. They took four days to make a complete inventory, in duplicate. One signed copy they handed to me, one they took away with them. A few days later officials returned with their copy marked in red ink, showing items and quantities now needed for use in the Army hospitals which had none. The items asked for were about 40% of the whole. They emphasized they were in no way trying to cripple our work, but they were asking for items which we held in excess of our needs. I knew this to be substantially true. I replied 'All right, you are now the Government here and are seeking to help the people. I will do as instructed.' I proceeded at once to get my staff on to the job of selecting the wanted items and putting them ready for transport. I do not think that I ever got so many black looks from my own friends and colleagues. 'He has thrown in his hand; this is the end of the hospital,' they murmured among themselves. But they did as I asked and next morning the things were removed as arranged. I stood silently, supervising, as they were carried out. By this action we proved to the new authorities' own satisfaction that we were giving real public service, by the way we had cared for this mass of uninvoiced potential wealth, and then by quietly and efficiently releasing it at their request. I am quite sure that nothing that I did in all those months was more worthwhile. It went a long way towards building up a feeling of confidence which enabled us quietly to continue our Christian witness right up to the time of our going. Perhaps I may also add that after it was all over Mary said to me that she had never been more proud of any action of mine than on that difficult day.

Wanted by the Police

During the whole of our twenty months after 'Liberation', we were constantly being sent for by the police, at any time of day or night, often entailing a long walk across town in the hot sun.

161

Throughout the time I was able to carry on my usual medical work without hindrance. In the beginning there was no interference in our church or social contacts with our friends. In later months our friends seemed to begin to avoid us, though we could still go to church. Afterwards we found that there had been a press proclamation ordering everyone to avoid all contact with 'Imperialists'. Anyone who was seen talking to us was to be immediately suspect. But our real friends did still find ways and means.

Usually when we went for one of these police examinations, Mary and I went together. When we arrived we were seated, one by one, at a small table with the main examiner facing us across the table. A second official close by took copious notes of everything that was said. Questioning was never too severe, often very routine and very boring. Questions like 'Why are you here?' 'What are you doing everyday?' 'What is your past history?' 'What schools did you attend?' 'Name them,' etc., following one another with, from time to time, a direct refusal to accept the answer given and a request for a different answer.

During our months of waiting two very unnecessary police investigations caused us endless bother and possibly contributed to hold us up, although my court trial was probably the greatest delaying factor.

The Photo Case

Without any special thought Mary and Gertrude had been taking a final film of snaps round the hospital and sent it to be developed in town, where a passing soldier spotted it as the work of a spy. I was sent for and told that I was responsible for what the women had done, and more and more questioning ensued. Not till many weeks had passed were Mary and I sent for again, but on arrival we were kept waiting in the police gatehouse as the Questioning Room was still occupied with some Roman Catholic priests. As we waited, an officer whom we had seen previously, passed us on his way to his office and saw us as he passed. Very soon he sent for us, and we were conducted far inside the building to his inner sanctum. He was evidently 'Top Brass'. As we entered he politely asked us to be seated and even offered us cigarettes, the acme of politeness among Red officials in those days, saying as he did so, 'It's nice to see you two old folks here. We know of all the work you have been doing for the poor of this town in the past years.' He then proceeded to return to us all the impounded photos. He merely asked me to sign the usual form of confession-receipt and dismissed us with every sign of good feeling.

162

We came out of that interview feeling very different from what we felt going in. Our medical work had been really appreciated by a responsible Red leader. We noted, however, that this was the only police interview that we ever had in Shaoyang when we were alone with an executive officer who had no writer or witness to check his actions.

The Camera Case

About the same time a quite separate rumpus developed around my own camera. While at work in hospital I had left the camera on my study desk at home. Mary was in the house all the time. A visiting policeman had come, had walked in despite mild protests from our cook, Hsiung ssu-fu, gone into the study and had taken (or stolen) the camera, which he knew I had from a previous visit. Mary did not actually see him but she heard his movements. The camera was gone and a few letters which had been propped against it were now lying flat on the desk. Mary at once, challenged the man about the camera but without result

Later a party came investigating but as it included the suspected man it only confused the issue. Again we were sent for, but I never felt able to make a complaint, as it might be that he was acting within his revolutionary rights!

Finally, one day a high-up officer appeared to consult me about an eye complaint. Only when we were alone did it transpire that he was really investigating this affair. He asked for a full account of everything. He also interviewed our two servants. He told me to send a full written account to his own head office and *not* to the local police. However, my letter was intercepted at the local police office and never reached him. I had to write it all again. And even my second letter was apparently delayed until I produced my receipt for it from the police gatehouse. As Mary said, there was some hanky-panky going on.

We heard no more of all this, nor did I get my camera back, but the offending man was, I think, moved elsewhere. After all this we learned to live without photographs in Revolutionary China!

Trial before a Communist Court of First Instance

My court case caused a long delay. It is a long story.

Some years before the Red Army arrived I had operated on the wife of one of the hospital servants, Yao by name. His wife had been brought to me having a very difficult obstructed labour. By opera-

163

tion (Symphysiotomy) both her own life and that of the baby were saved, but when she went home there was some residual weakness and a difficulty in walking following the operation.

During the early Communist reforms, a cell meeting of our coolies discovered that Yao had been cheating them all, by dishonest buying of the daily foods used in the hospital kitchen. He was reported to the Party and the police. After investigation, the Party called a big meeting of all the hospital workers and staff. Yao was stood up in front of this assembly and ordered to confess his sins against society for all to hear. He did so, repeating the words put into his mouth, thereby losing very much face. This accomplished, the authorities announced that he was not to be dismissed for he had confessed his errors.—'If he leaves you now he will be an outcast in society. He must be saved for society and re-habilitated. He must be given a job and begin from the bottom. You must reclaim him in your community and he must work out his salvation the hard way.' As Yao left the meeting he was heard to say he would get even with this 'hospital-show'. The only means he could find to do this was by bringing a legal case against myself, saying that my operation had ruined his wife's health. He duly made the charge and it was taken up by the People's Court. The Court made a most detailed investigation of the whole case. They got X-rays, signed medical opinions from outside and statements from everyone, but did not hold any open hearing. After some months of this enquiry, I was sent for to hear the verdict read. The judge was a young girl; I still possess her written judgement. In brief it says: 'A Poor Peasant has been injured and is unable to work properly. Doctor Pearson who operated on her has a good reputation but in this case he was at fault, and he should learn to operate better. We therefore order him to pay to the wife of Yao the sum of J.M.P. two hundred thousand dollars, (equivalent at that time to about £30).'

This was a mild judgement and could have been worse. I had the right of appeal to a higher court, with good prospect of success (as with Doctor Cundall in a parallel case in the Hankow Courts) but this would have meant more months of delay. Mary and Gertrude were worried by the already long delay. As I was able to find the money I therefore paid the fine and was duly acquitted.

Money might have been a great difficulty for us in those final weeks: what with the X-ray payment and 'back-pay' for coolies. When I got really short, and no money coming from England, strangely enough I was allowed to telegraph to Mr Richardson in Hankow, our only remaining missionary in Central China, and he was able to transfer to me, via the main Communist bank, a sum of money sufficient for all our final needs. This arrived almost next day by telegraphic transfer. All this inside a completely Communist economy! Our God does work in a mysterious way.

The Great Accusation Meeting

On April, 15th, 1951, the local Party officials summoned a great Mass Meeting, to meet in the hospital grounds at midday. It was a Sunday. We only learned about it quite casually the day before when men arrived to fix up flag poles and a stage on our lawn. Also many inflammatory paper placards and posters were strung up all over the grounds and even on our own house walls. In screaming headlines they shouted 'English, get out'. 'Down with the Imperialists'. 'Imperialists, go home'. And this at a time when we were doing our very best to be allowed to go home! Apparently the idea behind it all was to warn the people of our 'evil influence' as Europeans or 'Capitalists and Imperialists', and to encourage everyone to stand up and 'Speak out' if they had any grudge against us. Such assemblies could at times develop badly and get quite out of control.

We ourselves received no instructions about it, so next morning, well before the crowds were due, Mary and I went together out of the front gate, past the nurse-sentry on duty, telling her that we were going to Sunday morning service as usual. They could find us there if needed. We were allowed to pass unhindered. Gertrude Hughes stayed on duty in the wards.

Crowds soon flooded the compound. All the official agitators made their prepared speeches and a number of our own friends were compelled to say what they could about the subject in hand. One of these, we know, when forced to speak said something like this: 'I know this Doctor Pearson. I feel that he has for long tried to help the poor and the sick of this town. He should be left to carry on his work.' With this brave speech and with many others trying to say as little hurtful as possible, but with plenty of noise, the meeting passed over. A very heavy shower of rain towards its close helped it to disperse and washed away the thin paper posters.

But our Church service was over long before the mass meeting finished. This was the occasion when Mrs Shao, our minister's wife just out of prison herself, invited us to come and sit in her little home until the noise was over, and then provided us with a tasty little meal that I shall never forget.

When we got home I immediately sensed that our Christian friends were at bottom pleased with the result, for none of the

165

speakers had shown any new grounds for interference with us. I never heard just what resolutions had been passed. It does seem however, on looking back, that this meeting marked a sort of watershed and that thereafter official restrictions on our life and work increased.

Mary notes with humour that, after the rain had washed away nearly all the meeting posters, two, pasted on the brick walls of our house, remained sheltered by the overhanging eaves. These greatly annoyed her. We used to go out under cover of darkness and throw buckets of water at them, until they too, gradually 'weathered away'.

Suspicion Everywhere

Following the Accusation Meeting, in various ways things did begin to get more difficult for us, especially for Mary, often alone in the house when I was in hospital. It was about this time that our best Chinese friends began to be unable to call on us or even to be seen talking to us in the street. Everywhere we were now objects of suspicion, and we never knew what might happen next.

Mary herself, left some account of things from her point of view. I write what follows mostly from her memories.

A Search

On the Monday night after the big Meeting, April 16, we had both retired for the night. Gertrude was then in our spare room as her house had already been 'handed over'. Presently we heard shufflings on our front steps and a loud knock on the door. Thinking it was just a hospital night-call I looked out to enquire what was wanted. To my surprise, I saw a large group, coolies, students and younger staff members, demanding that I open the door to them. I put on my dressing gown and let them in. They then said they had come to search the house and especially all the baggage already packed for our journey to England. They allowed me to go upstairs to find my keys, and I warned Mary and Gertrude. But a nurse student was at once 'on duty' in each of their rooms and refused to let them even get out of bed. Meanwhile each room had its searchers and everything was opened and appraised. In desperation Mary did manage to sit up in bed and get her dressing gown and then started to read the only book at hand, a copy of the Psalms, her sentry gradually becoming a little more relaxed and friendly. I suppose they were mainly looking for firearms and wireless apparatus, neither of which we had. They also wanted to prevent us taking away any 'ancient objects of art' and the like, which they had been told Imperialists liked to steal from China. We had had one or two oldish bronze

166

vases, but knowing the general suspicions we had long ago given them away to Chinese friends.

Everything having been searched to their satisfaction, though at least one box was missed, they announced that they had found several items that might be 'ancient' and therefore 'illegal'—blessed word. These were being taken to the police office.

The sequel to all this occurred next afternoon, when some of the nurse students came up to see Gertrude, bringing back all the things which they had removed. They apologized and asked her to excuse them for what they had done, as the police had told them that none of these things were of any special historical value and were not 'illegal'. We might keep them. Gertrude replied that 'She was sure they had only done it to help us'. But when she suggested they take my articles back to me in person, they begged to be excused. Would she please take them to me? Apparently they did not mind 'loss of face' with her, but would rather not confess again to myself. Neither they nor we ever mentioned the matter again, and we remained all packed up till we left in August.

One day, perhaps a month or more before we left, one of the ward sisters warned Gertrude not to go for walks on the hills around the hospital in case we were taken for spies. Another sister came to see me, ostensibly on hospital business. That being concluded she stayed to say 'Please do not do any more major operations, as certain people are looking for an opportunity to accuse you and get you arrested'. Miss Wen was always friendly, especially with Gertrude, but she told us that, for the sake of the church she must not come round to see us any more, assuring us at the same time of her unchanged affection. For some weeks we did not leave the compound except to go to Morning Service on Sundays. How it did warm our hearts to be with them on those occasions, though Mary and I just took back seats.

In hospital during these last weeks I no longer had any Superintendent duties, but I was asked to continue my eye clinic every day and a number of other clinical duties came my way. I was reasonably busy. Gertrude likewise, had long ceased to have anything to do with duty-lists or store rooms, but to Mary it seemed there were still enough chances for things to go wrong at any minute and she was always on tenterhooks.

Worry—and Comedy

At one stage near the end, when we could think of no real reason for the continued hold-up of our departure, we thought it might be

167

that I alone was the one being held, and it might be possible for the ladies to go earlier if they went without me. We therefore got ready a Chinese language application for just the two ladies to leave. After a further ten weeks' wait Mary and Gertrude decided to go to the police by themselves and try to get things moving. Mary writes: 'We put on our dingiest garments and made no attempt at a hair-do. Gertrude darkened her eyes and we planned to look very miserable and to tell our sad tales . . . Just one man interviewed us. He said he understood our difficulties. It would be in order for us to leave but that George was still held pending the law judgement. But he supposed we would all three like to travel together? We asked how soon we might expect the judgement—in another week or two?' 'Oh, not so long as that,' he replied. So back we went without proceeding further, knowing how glad George would be, yet hardly daring to hope. We had been so often disappointed.'

'A week passed and still no word,' continues Mary. 'I began to go off the deep end and to declare that it was 'all words' once again. But then we got the judgement, as illustrated and told elsewhere. George was sent for by the police once again and our tummies turned over because one never knew what was up. But it was to tell him that the permits could now be granted for all three! There were still some days of further delay because of the needed advertisements in the papers to announce our departure and of the almost impossibility of our making contacts with the printers in Changsha. But in the end the advert. did appear and that very same day the police fixed August 6th, only two days ahead, for our departure. We had been waiting for nine months.'

Even then there was almost a hold-up. I had mis-read some printed Chinese instructions and got to the police station only just in time to get the passes, because one of our male nurses—a providential angel—happened to read through the document and show me my mistake.

I should perhaps add that in these final days we repeatedly found that the local police were most helpful, smoothing things out and actually preventing ardent hot-heads like our cow-boy from putting up fresh obstacles to our movements.

CHAPTER NINETEEN

Going . . .

The Shaoyang Church says its Good-bye to us

IT WAS during our last weeks in Hunan, when we were living under the new regime that it happened that the Red Flag, which our church congregation had had to buy for ceremonial display, was stolen. This could have been serious for the church. The members therefore decided to collect money to buy a new one.

With this highly 'correct' object in view, a small party of workers and members boldly came to our house despite all prohibitions of contact with 'Imperialists'. They brought their collecting book so as to 'demand' from us a subscription, a very proper proceeding. Once inside, however, the collecting party became a real Methodist Class Meeting and a farewell from them to us. They freely spoke their thanks and their love for us, and their prayers, told us of their own difficulties.

With a small contribution to their flag fund duly entered in their collecting book (as a proof of what they had been doing) they were gone.

That was our last unfettered contact with our Chinese friends. They did not dare even to be seen speaking to us in the streets at this time. Before they went they specially asked us not to try to write any letters to them after we left, nor must we expect any letters from them. Any such would be intercepted by the censors and would only got them into trouble. 'But', they continued, 'please pray for us, and we will pray for you. Do not fear for this Church. It is our Church now. You brought us this Bible and its message. You gave us these buildings. The job is ours now. We are the church here. We will carry on.'

Such was their final message to us and to the church which had sent us, spoken during those last few days in Shaoyang.

As I write this in 1967 we still have no direct message, but we believe they do carry on. A refugee message in 1964 told us: 'All your friends are well.'

We May Go. August 1951

Not until nine months after our definite application to be allowed to leave Shaoyang did that final permit arrive, and then we had to be gone in two days! What a time of waiting this had been, especially for Mary. One or two extracts from her letters perhaps, give a glimpse of what it had meant for her. As early as October 1950 she

169

had written: 'For a woman of my years I feel ridiculously impatient, but I know that the next few months will pass and I have plenty to do.' Actually she made jobs to do. One such was the making of two new pairs of pyjamas for me, entirely hand-sewn, as she then had no sewing machine. Her 'few months' dragged on and on.

In May 1951 she wrote to our daughter Eleanor: 'As I walked in the garden this morning I was praying for two things. One was for a letter to tell me that your little Eliz was better, and that news has come today. The other was for the way to open soon for us to come to you.'

That May she also unexpectedly found herself called upon to address the Quarterly Meeting of the Shaoyang Church, under its Chairman Rev. Chang Mou-sheng, a vigorous man fully alive to the dangers and opportunities of the time. She continues: 'I really felt very unfit for the task, but I supposed I would not have been asked if they had thought that I could not do it. I made use of Hugh Martin's 'Portrait of Jesus'. It meant a lot of hard work in all my available sitting-down time last week. In the end I managed . . . and held forth for forty-five minutes. The actual thinking out of the Chinese phraseology, and looking up verses took a good deal of time.' It was really wonderful what command Mary did have of the language considering all the family interruptions from those early years and long war years at home.

Before we could leave all our luggage had to be unpacked and inspected by the 'Hospital Guard', consisting mostly of our own student nurses. After that the police themselves came round and did it all again. They then sealed every package to ensure that there was no more unofficial searching by self-appointed squads.

Farewells

The day before we left Shaoyang one of our comrades in the work at hospital actually dared to call at our front door, carrying some patients' records sheets and to ask for medical orders. But it was soon evident that this too was a goodbye call. A colleague who had been in England specially wanted to send thanks to all who had helped so much one who was away from home and who had been ill there. A certain typewriter might be found in Hong Kong and sold, and a small present of real Chinese tea taken to each friend who had helped. This I was able to carry through as we passed through Hong Kong. This, rather than that scurrilous letter, surely showed the real feelings of many friends whom we left behind.

Even as we were going to bed about midnight, that last night, our cow-boy came pushing in with a demand that I must pay for milk used during the past three days, even though it was from our own cows. Fortunately I still had a little loose cash around, and he disappeared, satisfied that he had done his duty.

At dawn we were off, walking almost silently to the bus station. Our best friends did not dare to come to see us off, but some stood in their doorways as we passed, by arrangement, but giving no outward sign. We knew what they meant. Only one or two 'poor peasant' coolies whom we knew were able to move around to see what was happening and say a furtive farewell.

And so we left Shaoyang on what was at home August Bank Holiday morning, 1951, after being a part of it for thirty-one years.

We reached Changsha without incident and, still under police direction, we were assigned to stay in a small inn in the city for a night or two until we could get our tickets to Canton. We were of course, quite cut off from our then Chairman. In fact, friends had advised me not to try to see him or to say any sort of official good byes. I did however, manage to write a brief note of farewell. He wrote no reply but I am sure both he and I understood.

The following day we were still held up in the city so I walked round to say goodbye to a family of German C.I.M. missionaries in the city. I found them and whilst I was talking to the German doctor, a friend must have gone to a Chinese lady whom I knew well, asking her to come at once. I shall never forget her look of surprise as she came to the door of the room where we were talking. I think that Mary and Gertrude Hughes were with me. 'Doctor Pearson!' was all that she could say. She came in and there in that friendly German home we were able to talk freely. I was able to give her details of the final disposal of church funds remaining in my hands, the care of the Christian missionary graves, and make a final hand over. She took our goodbyes to the Changsha Christians and gave us theirs. Then together with our German friends we knelt in prayer. So brief, yet so heartfelt, and a time of parting and uncertainty for us all.

She left by the door through which she had come. We waited a little with our friends, and then we walked out, our host coming with us to the main street gate.

We had said our last goodbye to the church in Hunan. This was the very last contact that we were able to make with our greatly loved Chinese colleagues. Our little party were the very last of our English missionary workers in Hunan. Next morning we were on the train for home. But the Chinese Church still carries on.

About twenty-four hours of rail travel brought us to Canton City. How Mary and Gertrude did rejoice when they could get a real hair-do at a Chinese European-style barber's shop. Again there were more baggage examinations and a night in an hotel before we could get on the train for Hong Kong. A Red customs officer from Hunan who knew of our work, made final formalities easier and we were soon crossing the footbridge over the border stream.

Friends were waiting on the British side of the border to welcome us. I had to find a tailor at once to get some respectable clothes. I must have been thin, as the suit I then had made was much too small for me after a few months on home diet. But what a shock it was to us after all that time in New China to see the terrible poverty flaunting itself everywhere on the Hong Kong streets, together with the excessive luxury of so many both Europeans and Chinese in Rolls Royce cars and huge houses. Communist Chinese may justly boast that such extremes no longer exist in their land.

A Glance Back

And so we had left China! In our early days we had seen something of the corruption and the selfishness of the old society now being ousted. We had lived through many years of a changing political situation, the long-drawn years of the selfish mis-rule of the War Lords, when the common people had no voice, but were harrassed and oppressed by landlords and money-lenders. I suppose that in many cases it was literally true that they had little to lose by an overthrow of authority but their chains.

This situation was one which we missionaries had mostly quite failed to see, or if we did get a glimpse into it, we felt that it was not a situation with which we, as outsiders, could or should interfere. Perhaps we saw only one side of a many-sided complex. We saw a spiritual need and we saw the need of individuals whom we met and whom we tried to help. Schools and hospitals were needed as well as the Gospel of Love, and these we gave. For years our institutions were way ahead, until we were overtaken by government finance and power.

Mao Tse tung, a local man from nearby Siangtan in Hunan, who had gone through the Government Normal School at Changsha, had early sensed something of the economic and political needs of the peasant folk around him. For 20 years he read all he could get hold of, studied, talked and listened to the stories of wrongs and oppression. Later he worked and plotted for the new day of com-munal self-help. For years he advocated working with the Kuoming-

172

tang organizations, but later found them too conservative and tradition bound. His methods were ruthless. He fought both friend and foe as he tried to sow the seeds of the new ideas in the minds of his people.

It was a classic revolutionary situation the Chinese people found themselves in. Mao and a few dedicated revolutionaries set out to use it and to build a new society. Through their years in opposition they must have built up a superb organization. Their methods were absolutely ruthless and included violence and the literal elimination of all opposition. But there must still have been some other factor making for the success of their revolution. One still wonders at the way in which so many of the common people accepted and did all that they were told. Living as we did amongst them, it was almost uncanny to see the spread, like a prairie fire, of the new thought and ideas. Was it a use of mass psychology? Or just plain hysteria? Things were accomplished which to us on the spot, had seemed quite impossible a few months earlier, and many of them were very good things too.

To begin with it was largely a revolution built on the text books of Marx, Engels, Lenin and Stalin, which were being studied and followed everywhere. Mao's own works were not far behind and were soon in front, as he showed the need to diverge from the old Russian reliance on the 'Town Proletariat', to a reliance on the 'poor peasants' of his own countryside. 'We have no such town proletariat in China,' he said.

In Russia as I had seen it from the inside thirty years earlier, the pre-revolutionary situation had been very different. The old society had suddenly collapsed as the enormous defeated Russian armies struggled home. Into this utter confusion Lenin had arrived and he succeeded in imposing his own ideas of what should be done, in that very fluid situation. The Russian reconstruction was almost spontaneous, working out *de novo* what was needed. The Chinese reconstruction was largely a following out of the route plotted in the paper backs from Russia, from Germany, from Spain and elsewhere, but with adaptations to Chinese life.

How I Saw It

To me, as to many of those who had been working in China and for the Chinese people for many years, the new regime had been a constant puzzle. We were always being told of, and we appreciated, its high aims. We saw some of its successes as it sought to liberate its people from an age-old economic slavery. We saw its self-

173

assurance and its conviction that its methods were really the only way out. It did so much good for the common man, that many thoughtful people were saying: 'Let them be. Let us see what they can do.' Yet at the same time, all around us we saw the stark cruelty and mercilessness of its methods against its opponents and against those formerly in power. Many thousand such were shot in cold blood, (like the elimination of the Jews under Hitler) and very many more educated and presumably useful members of society were left in an extremity of hopelessness, useless and unwanted in the new world in which they found themselves. For many of these suicide seemed the only way out, many others, when the chance offered, fled, leaving everything behind. Still others, and this included the majority of China's Christians, stayed behind and bravely tried to see the good things, the best in the new way of life, and to come to terms with it. Such men are the salt of the earth. Of such men is the Church in China today.

For myself then, whilst approving most of the aims and much of the accomplishment of the Revolution, as a Christian I could never co-operate in its methods, either in Russia or later in China. Was it after all the same difficulty which I had felt at home when in war time, I had felt unable to co-operate with our own Government in its war methods?

It is never easy to be a Christian. Our job in China was to serve those in need, as and when we could, passing on the message, giving the reasons for our actions as opportunity offered.

The Church? In 1901 there were no Christians in Hunan. In 1965. even after 16 years of Communist rule, there is still a Christian Church in many places in China. Small it may be, but both real and deeply sincere. (What has happened since 1965 during all the Red Guard agitations and disturbances we do not know. Many church buildings may have been forcibly closed?)

We do know that the hospital we built, functions today as the County hospital for Shaoyang. It is run largely by our own pupils, still serving their own people of that vast countryside. How I wish I could hear again from some of those busy fellow-workers and friends.

CHAPTER TWENTY

Retirement? Get up and Go

I HAD ALWAYS expected and hoped that I might serve the whole of my working life in China. But it was not to be. When Mary and I returned home in 1951 I had already passed the age of sixty. She was over fifty-eight and still liable to her recurring attacks of depression. It was thus now hardly possible for us to go to some new work abroad. I therefore needed to find a job at home. This was the time when every general practice vacancy in the British National Health Service was attracting about 60 applicants. At sixty-one I hardly stood a chance. For six months I answered *B.M.J.* advertisements and did occasional 'locums' to fill in time. Eventually it was to the small colliery village of Chasetown in South Staffordshire that we went, I as Assistant-with-view to Doctor C. R. Houghton, who had more work in his one-man practice than he could manage. After six months this developed into a very happy partnership. We had to take over an old house in the village, part of a row of terrace cottages which had been used by local doctors for generations past.

We soon began to learn something of the people and their Staffordshire dialect, where 'we' is used instead of 'our' and 'cor' instead of 'can't'. 'We likes we o'd ways. We cor be bothered wi' a' these new trankelments.'

I found that English patients suffer in much the same ways as had my patients in China. Some are nervy; some don't take the advice given; some get measles and some get cancer, etc. But in China we saw more preventable infectious diseases, due to primitive and insanitary living conditions.

But of our days in Chasetown I cannot now write at length. They are still too near and most of those involved are still with us. Days were busy, and night calls not infrequent. Both I and Mary were soon involved in the local Methodist Church work. This period of general practice lasted almost nine years. By and large it was a time of happy home life, with our growing family spreading its wings.

When, after some years at Chasetown, Mary developed signs of heart trouble, we found a nearby site and commenced the process of building a small bungalow to which to retire properly, and I gave notice that I would retire in the early summer of 1961. But that joint retirement was not to be, for it was in February 1961 when Mary passed away. She never saw the completed new home. It was our daughter Christine and I who moved in a few months later.

175

I prepared to begin a quieter life, in my garden and with my bees, violin and occasional church duties. I had not qualified for a N.H.S. pension, but had got a 'retirement grant' which with my small mission pension and the State Old Age Pension, meant that I could live quietly in comfort.

Summer 1961 was passing quietly and the land round our bungalow gradually began to look more like a garden. At such times thoughts come to one. Ought I ever to think of the possibility of remarriage? But no-one could ever fill the place of Mary in my life. And would not such a thought even, be disloyalty to her? She and I were still united in that great Christian hope of life with our Risen Lord, to which those last three words of hers—'yes, yes, yes'—gave such vivid expression. Yes, she would still be with me as I travelled the quiet road of retirement, I could still talk to her. I have dared to write thus because I feel that it gives the key to much that happened later. What follows is still very much a part of 'Our Story'.

Ghana?

I was sitting at my desk one morning, late in October 1961, my telephone rang: a trunk call for Dr. Pearson. Doctor Frank Davey of the Methodist Missionary Society, London, was speaking. 'Was I well? Yes, thank you. Was I doing any work? No, just gardening and collecting my O.A.P. Then could I help?'

A small hospital in Ghana was in trouble. They had no doctor. The hospital at Wenchi is a responsibility of the newly-independent Methodist Church in Ghana. They had appealed for help as, if they could not find qualified staff, Government might take over. Could London find them a doctor? Even for just three months, which would give them opportunity to look for their own man. Would I go for such a short service in Ghana Methodism?

This made me gasp! I had contemplated no such adventure. I said that I would think it over and pray round it. The result was that I could find no adequate excuse for not going. My home here would continue. Christine helped by saying she would take in a colleague as lodger for company. To make a short story shorter, ten days later I found myself landing from a B.O.A.C. Comet at Accra, being met there by the African President of the Ghana Methodist Church, the Rev. F. C. F. Grant.

Two days later, after having been a guest at the official Garden Party given by President Nkrumah for Queen Elizabeth at Christiansborg Castle, I was driven to Kumasi and next day on to Wenchi, an out-lying village in the Ashanti forest area, now the province of

176

Brong-Ahafo.

Wenchi is a village of about 6,000 people, amongst whom at least six languages are currently spoken, none predominating. In such a situation English remains the language of Government as of much else. The chiefs have dedicated a large plot of land just outside the village to the Mission, and on it stands a large church, the hospital of twenty-nine beds and O.P.D., etc., and also a large school. The hospital was begun some ten years earlier by a missionary on the spot, in partnership with the village Chief, but it has fallen on evil days and cannot get any doctor. The Ghana Methodist Church has promised to collect £500 a year and a Government grant of £12,000 a year is being paid. Such a large subsidy to a relatively small Mission hospital brings its own difficulties. People say that the hospital is a rich institution and should help in finding jobs for their needy relations!

I early discovered that the hospital had a big new operating theatre, recently erected but never used. All doors and windows had been removed and the building was going to rack and ruin. Gradually a sorry story revealed itself.

A large local gift had been given with the condition that it be administered by the Village Council. Elaborate plans had been drawn up by a mission architect, too elaborate for such a small hospital in my view, and work commenced. Half-way through, all the funds had dissapeared and the contractor was demanding his money. Some official investigation led to the imprisonment of the Village Council, and the contractor, seeing no chance of his money, had deliberately gone off with all the wooden doors and window glass, etc.

Things had settled a bit before I arrived. I was able to get a carpenter to make new doors and to buy glass from Accra. The architect's plans had stipulated for machinery for sterilizing by electricity and for a complete supply of hot and cold sterile water. Alas, there was (in that hot weather) no water supply at all except what came in buckets by cart; and even if we had had water, our small generator could not raise enough power to supply both sterilizers and normal lighting. Finally however, we got the theatre into use and for its proper purpose, though the water still came in country buckets. On the opening day a short service was held in the main operating room to dedicate it, to pray together and to remove if possible, some of the ill-will and corruption which had surrounded it.

There was a good Out-Patient building, treating perhaps eighty

177

people a day. When I officiated there I had a young nurse as interpreter. When we were ready for the next patient she would shout out his name in a very loud and shrill voice like a corncrake, though in person she looked just like the bust of Queen Nefertiti of Egypt.

Ward nursing was poor. The hospital did not provide food for patients, so that their relatives were always on the spot—so they did much of the nursing chores too. Discipline in the Nurses' Home was almost non-existent and morals often doubtful. As a Mission hospital it was not a shining success, but despite all, it did provide the only medical care available in the neighbourhood.

As the time of my three months appointment came to an end the Ghana Church was no nearer finding a successor. Instead, the State Health Authorities at my request sent up a well-qualified African Christian doctor. He arrived in his own Mercedes-Benz and with a Government salary four times that of a Mission doctor, and his doctor-wife is getting a similar salary elsewhere.

While in Wenchi I greatly enjoyed sharing in the happy home life of Peter and Kathleen Howard and their little family. At their local church, another very unfinished specimen of a building, I took my turn at taking the services, with an interpreter. The large congregation appeared in every conceivable variety of costume, from European tropical suits to the lovely brilliant coloured Ghana gown or 'cloth', or to rags and tatters. One day as I was leaving after service I was accosted by an inconspicuous African in European dress who wanted to talk. 'I am the M.P. for Wenchi,' he said. 'I want to thank you for all that you are doing for our people here . . .' and he went on to talk to me like a good Methodist Circuit Steward: 'We so value missionary service like yours because it is not done for money like the work of so many Government servants. I do hope that you will stay a long time in Wenchi. You must not leave us. Tell me what you want done and I will see to it.' I excused myself, saying that I was then over seventy and had duties elsewhere. 'Never mind' he replied, 'you still have strength to work for another four years at least.' That was one of the Nkrumah Party members speaking from his heart.

Also in Wenchi is the home of Kofi Bussia, a leading political opponent of Nkrumah then on United Nations Staff in New York, but a member of the same Methodist church in Wenchi.

The BBC takes a Hand. Hong Kong

Earlier in 1960, when I was still in practice at home and Mary a patient in hospital, two letters reached me from Hong Kong. The writers, whom I did not know, had only got my Chinese name and had written to Mission friends to try to identify me. It seemed that a former nurse pupil of ours in Shaoyang was now working in Hong Kong under her married name of Mrs Rose Tai. She graduated at Shaoyang in 1943, but her Chinese Government Certificate is not recognized in Hong Kong. She was doing very good work, could I help to get her fully recognized as the well-trained nurse that she was?

When Rose herself wrote, she hinted mysteriously about visiting England soon. Were we excited? At last, an opportunity to meet again one of our fellow-workers from Hunan. Rose was to come to England at BBC expense to interview a Miss Wilson, a Scottish nurse with whom she had been working in a refugee clinic in Hong Kong.

A few weeks later she stepped off a plane in London and it did not take her long to find her way to Chasetown. But Helen Wilson got herself a fractured leg and the broadcast was delayed and Rose eventually returned without broadcasting. For me however, the main result was that I learned at first hand of the work being done at the United Church Clinic for Refugees at Rennie's Mill outside Hong Kong. I also found that they needed a doctor for a year to allow their regular doctor, Helen Clow to get a furlough. The upshot of it all was that the Church of Scotland, unable to find a real Presbyterian doctor, took on a Methodist and sent me out to Hong Kong for a year, to take the place of Doctor Clow who is Baptist supported by the United Church of Canada!

Hong Kong—China Again

As our boat tied up at Kowloon Wharf, I saw Rose Tai with a crowd of nurses and others come to welcome me. Rose was the key to the excitement. In China, now as always, the relationship of teacher and student is one of vast importance. It is almost a parent-child relationship. Once 'My Teacher' always 'My Teacher', and Rose was welcoming her own old teacher to her own place of exile. No trouble was too much. It was all pure joy. I was whisked away along the ten mile route to Rennie's Mill in the clinic's Landrover. What a journey! First through town streets, and then along a narrow mountain road winding in all directions in and out of the narrow green valleys, more like giddy-go-round than a serious road. But we did get there.

Rennie's Mill

Long years ago a certain Mr Rennie had built a small cotton mill on a

179

site in Junk Bay between an arm of the harbour and the steep hillside. He had failed and his mill has long passed away. The place was derelict.

In 1949 came the great exodus of refugees from Red China, hundreds of thousands of them crowding into the small colony. In desperation the Hong Kong Government allowed 20,000 homeless wanderers to dump themselves on this empty site and on the surrounding hillside, where there was a small freshwater stream. They might build houses there if they could, and a soup-kitchen would provide one meal a day for the time being. Huts of every kind were soon run up, using any possible or impossible material—tin cans beaten flat, cardboard, sacks, stones, bamboos or brushwood. There were no streets, no plans, no lighting and no drainage. All water must be carried from the little stream. The suffering and squalor soon produced disease: intestinal infections, typhoid, cholera, tuberculosis, malnutrition and malaria were rife. The nearest hospital or doctor was ten miles away in town. They had no transport; they just suffered and died.

Through the years that have passed, the original huts have mostly been rebuilt as their owners found part-time jobs. They are now mostly rain-proof but still on the same sites, and in the same confusion and squalor.

Relief Comes

Into this tragedy came a small group of Christian nurses on an exploratory visit. Helen Wilson of the Scottish Church and Miss Tragardt of the Swedish Zion Mission. They saw the need. At an occasional repeat visit a clinic was held on a big rock on the seashore.

The nurses got local churches interested and a group of seven or eight different Hong Kong Churches formed a 'Junk Bay Relief Committee' to support a United Christian Clinic at Rennie's Mill. Funds were also sought from Church World Service, Christian Aid, Oxfam, etc., and a regular daily clinic came into being.

Apart from the acute infections, tuberculosis was soon recognized as a major problem to be tackled. In these small huts it spread like wild-fire through whole families. As the patients died they infected everyone else in their hut. What could be done? In faith, and out of their own pockets, the nurses hired a small hut with no other facilities and put a few dying patients into it, in an effort to prevent the infection of others. In the years since this small start twelve

180

years ago, there has now come into being the large modern 'Haven-of-Hope Sanitorium' with 260 beds, only half-a-mile from Rennie's Mill Village.

But the early medical workers found that many refugees were refusing to accept in-patient treatment in the Sanitorium. Why? Their reply was: 'But if we go into hospital who will care for and feed our children?' (Hong Kong has no Sick-pay or Unemployment Pay.) A small 'Children's Home' was therefore organized to take in the children of such parents during the months that father or mother was in hospital. A happy home it is. Our American friends have a name for it. They call it the 'Preventorium'. The House-father and House-mother are themselves Christian refugees from Hunan.

At Rennie's Mill I occupied a small Oxfam concrete flat built right amongst the refugee homes. I had to take the daily clinic and as most of the refugees could speak Mandarin Chinese, the language which we used in Hunan, I was at home again.

The head of nursing at the clinic was Isabelle Miller of Canada, but Rose Tai (nominally second-in-command) was in on everything. She could speak both Mandarin and Cantonese plus some English, and her unrivalled knowledge of these people and their difficult ways over the past ten years was of immense value. She was 'Mother' to all the young recently graduated nurse-aids who formed our staff. She could tell them off when necessary, teach them, work with them, do the housekeeping, and she regularly and most acceptably took prayers. She had an ability to talk straight in their own idiomatic way, telling them the truth in love.

The Children

To me it was the children who were the wonder of this village. They swarmed. They played everywhere. Very many of the original refugees of twelve years ago had died off. Their children remained. I estimated that perhaps 50% of the people today in Rennie's Mill are under twelve. Born since their parents left China. Mission schools have multiplied. The Catholics have 1,800 pupils in their Middle School. The Norwegians 1,300 in their big Girls' Middle School and there are several other Chinese foundations and even a small Buddhist school. Many are functioning though still unregistered. At a National Youth Festival in Rennie's Mill I actually counted between 3,000 and 4,000 children in procession all from local Middle Schools, and the official estimate for the total village population is now about 10,000. School-teacher is now the commonest occupation.

181

One sees children everywhere. Gaily dressed girls wearing the latest summer dresses from parcels of clothing from England or U.S.A., or in winter the lovely woollies, and they make really good use of them. Nowadays the Chinese girls have their lovely straight black hair carefully permed so that abundant curls are the rule, and make-up is plentiful. For the teenagers modern fashions now extend to boy-girl relationships. Most of the Middle Schools are co-ed. They read the latest glossies and walk around arm-in-arm. How my old Chinese friends in Hunan would be scandalized! Happily, high heels have not yet found their way into Rennie's Mill. Perhaps their steep hill paths account for that.

Th e Refugees—Old Friends

On my second day at Rennie's Mill I was walking along the narrow street when I was suddenly greeted by name in Chinese by a passing Chinese pedestrian! 'Pi I-Sheng' he called out. He was a refugee who had known me in Shaoyang where I had actually operated on his wife! What a welcome I got. He was not long in rounding up other Shaoyang refugees who came in a group to my flat to greet me. They were thrilled. Half-a-dozen were former patients who could proudly show their old operation scars as their proof of former acquaintance. Now we were all together again in a strange land, all refugees together, myself included.

Nothing would do but they must arrange a feast of welcome for me. In this setting it was never a case of 'What can you give to us poor refugees?' Rather was it: 'What can we do for you?' Surely it must be a unique experience to meet thus, quite by accident, people whom one has known perhaps twenty or thirty years earlier, in very different place and circumstances, and out of a population of perhaps 600,000,000.

All have suffered much in the intervening years. All feel bitterly about being so completely cut off from their old homes by the Red censorship. Several are ex-military officers of the old China Armies and still have an exaggerated loyalty to Chiang Kai-shek and the Taiwan 'Government in Exile'. They display Taiwan flags on every possible occasion. They find it hard to accept their new poverty and are often a thorn in the side of the Hong Kong local authorities. They dislike regulations and modern management.

So the feast was held and one or two of my European friends invited to keep me company. A few weeks later I was able to return the compliment and throw a feast for them. But the day before I finally left they again invited me out, and that time I had no opportunity to repay my debts.

Other unexpected happenings emphasized this feeling that I was 'at home' in Rennie's Mill. As I was a whole year there one day was my birthday. No one knew, but foolishly, after I had finished the morning clinic I let out the secret in conversation with the nurse on duty. After tea that evening, I was asked to meet the nurses. And they then and there presented me with a lovely Parker pen inscribed with my name, age and date, and a proverb wishing me long life.

Only a few weeks later a cheap pen that I had been using disappeared from my desk in the clinic while my back was turned. The nurses were worried; I said it did not matter. Two mornings later there was a strange pen in my desk. 'Someone else had lost his pen,' I said. 'Oh no,' replied the nurse on duty, 'that is your pen, we want you to have it.' What more could I say but mutter my unworthy thanks. Such was the atmosphere in which I lived during those months in Hong Kong.

After I had returned to England I had many letters from these fellow workers. One I reproduce here because I feel that the writer, Rosalie Chung, a young nurse, has caught something of the atmosphere of the teacher-student situation which Rose Tai so conspicuously showed. I retain Rosalie's quaint English. She uses the word 'love' in its true Christian sense. It is a joy of a letter.

R.M. Church Clinic
Dec. 3rd. 1963.

'Dear Dr. Pearson,

I am very sorry that I have not write to you since you leave us. Many times when I took my pen and paper to send my best wishes to you, that I cannot decided weather I should write in English or in Chinese, so poor my English is.

'Here in the Clinic all things go on as usual, except we like Doctor together (i.e. to be here). Indeed deep in my heart I cannot forget that I have been working with a Chinese-Old-Man-like-Doctor. You know a Chinese youth respected the aged people, same in my hart, I love you as well as I love my grandfather, and this love only the Chinese and those who have lived in China for a long time can understand.

'Doctor, I have dug out all my English from my mind and put them in this paper. I hope I can dug out my English more next times

183

and write to you.' (Then, in Chinese) 'May our God bless you with rest and happiness. My friend Mr Yip (her fiance) asks after you.
Yours sincerely,
Rosalie Chung.'

In Hong Kong I met again Dr John Chen Hsi-Min, now a senior surgeon at the large Queen Mary Hospital. He was for a time on the staff at Shaoyang, up to the time of the Japanese invasion. Now, in his very important post in Hong Kong he still carries out his work in a real spirit of Christian service to the poorest, which (he freely states) he first learned during his time with us in Hunan. His joy is to be able to serve those who can pay nothing. As he took me round his wards I could see how his patients loved and trusted him.

New Buildings
Whilst at Rennie's Mill I found time to draw up plans for a new Clinic building to replace the old Government-owned shed which the Clinic was using and which had been destroyed by a typhoon just before I had arrived.

My plans were submitted by the Relief Committee to the Government Health Department and thence on to the official architects. They were approved in every detail, and improved structurally, and a very substantial grant was voted for the scheme before I left.

Since I left I have had photos of the fine new Clinic building built to my outline plans. It includes six beds for emergency cases, a large lecture room for Public Health work, consulting rooms, X-ray operation room, sterilizing rooms, dressing rooms, nurses' rooms, laboratory and even a laundry. It is a wonderful boon to the work and will eventually, if Relief work ceases, become a full local Government Health Centre.

News from Inside China
This is still very hard to get. I tried hard to find what my refugee friends knew of their homes, but almost always drew a blank. They got no news beyond rare family messages.

Rose Tai's old father and mother (he is a retired Lutheran pastor) are still in their Hunan home. They are able to send out an occasional brief letter of greeting and sometimes a photo of themselves looking happy and well, has come through the post. Their letters *never* contain any general news.

It was not till I was home again in England that one refugee wrote to me saying that, in response to his enquiries he had had a letter

184

from a brother in Shaoyang. A message for me said: 'All your friends in Shaoyang are well. A certain doctor (name) is now (1963) head of the hospital, which is now the County hospital.' That was all, but my refugee friend added: 'Do you know any doctor of this name?' I should think I do know him! He is the Christian doctor who took over when I left. I know that he has had a far from easy time. It is indeed *great news* that he and other friends and fellow workers are still carrying on the tradition of service, and that the buildings which we erected are still in use and of service to the people of the area.

Kenya

I was home again. It was late 1963 and my telephone rang again. The result? In January I flew to Nairobi.

A small Methodist hospital at Maua in Kenya was suddenly left without a doctor. A new appointment could not be ready for at least three months; I was to act till then.

I was met at the airport by old China friends, Rev. and Mrs Elliott Kendall, also Peter and Shirley Deakin. Peter is an R.A.F. technician posted in Nairobi and a keen worker in the English-speaking church there. Next morning I was sent off early by taxi for the 150 mile trip to Meru and the next day on to Maua. It is a trip through wonderful country. Much of it is open grazing land where one casually meets zebra, gazelles or ostriches beside the road. Later the road runs amid steep hills and valleys. The ever-white snow-capped summit of Mount Kenya, almost on the Equator, is only a few miles away.

Maua is a small village in the old Native Reserve of the Meru people, nearly 6,000 feet above sea-level. Life in the area is very primitive. Most homes are still the old round huts, built of sticks and mud with a thatch roof. The people still live by their old-style subsistence agriculture in their 'gardens' and with their poor thin cattle. Women do all the hard work. The men seem to have no manual skills. In the old days all had to train as tribal braves, but not now. So what can they do? The new world all around them is often hard to understand.

I found myself in a busy little 90 bed hospital, which is loved and trusted by all the people around. It carried on its work all through the difficult Mau-Mau emergency years, undefended, though the dreaded raiders were known to be in the forest, not far away. Many whites and Christians had been killed, but the hospital was never harmed.

185

Out-patients were allowed to attend at any time for treatment, a peculiar survival of the days before clocks, but it leads to desultory staff work. A curious local custom is that a patient who is very ill is often brought to hospital by his friends and then left to die comfortably, his family returning to the forest. One Meru man told me that 'In the old days we used to take our sick ones out into the forest to die. Now we bring them to the hospital instead.' Whilst I was in Maua, the village headman and his council dedicated a special plot of land for the 'hospital funerals'.

Maua Hospital has its own system of chlorinated running water, set up by a former superintendent. It also has a septic-tank drainage system—which sometimes works!

A School of Nursing trains well-qualified Nurse Aids, who are always in great demand.

I Meet Mau-Mau

I had hardly been in Maua for a week when I had a strange experience, meeting the acknowledged leaders of the very recent Mau-Mau rebellion, now known as the Forest Freedom Fighters.

It was on Saturday January 18th, 1964. A big meeting had been arranged on the local village Stadium. The Mau-Mau leaders would come. All day long the drums had been sounding, but the expected guests were very late. Towards evening a message reached me that they would also like to address the hospital staff! I duly invited them. It was after 8 p.m. when the deputation in its four old cars reached the hospital. We assembled in the small O.P.D. waiting room. 'They' had come!

They were a party of ten to fifteen people. Among them was 'Field Marshal' Mwariama, for long a leader of the Forest Mau-Mau, six feet tall, with staring eyes and his hair in tousled knots. (Only a few days earlier I had seen him on home television at the Kenya Independence Celebrations with the Duke of Edinburgh and others.) He and his party sat at a table facing us in the dark room, fitfully illuminated by oil lamps, all of us on straight backless benches. One of our male nurses, Mr Stanley, acted as chairman-interpreter.

When Mwariama rose to speak he used Swahili, not the local Kimeru. He spoke in a quiet conversational way, a pleasant smile often passing over his tense face. Stanley translated into English. The burden of the speech was: 'We are now at peace. It is our duty to love one another. Black and white all alike. We must serve one another and we must all work for our country, the new Kenya. We have come today to ask for your co-operation.'

The next speaker was a woman, the widow of Dedan Kimathi. Her late husband had been supreme 'Field Marshal' of the rebels, but had been betrayed, captured and shot by the British Forces. She was a small woman and was dressed in rough soldier's uniform, like a Communist cadre. She also spoke of the need for love and for working together. At one point she noticed my white hair and pointed to me saying, 'You must all grow old in service like that old man'. Later she became somewhat bitter in her remarks, pointing to some inferior clothing used by patients. Perhaps one can understand her bitterness. Kimathi had been an active fighter and had killed many Africans and Europeans. She must since have been trained in Russia, for when they were leaving she said goodbye to me in perfect Russian, '*dosvidania*'.

She was followed by a polished young educated African, now an M.P. in Nairobi. With these men was a motley bodyguard of fighters, rough, tough men, looking rather dazed in the lamplight. Fighters, rough, tough men, looking rather dazed in the lamplight. Several of them were introduced as 'Generals'.

Our own Mr Henry also spoke. He had been Head Assistant and Local Preacher for 36 years. He lived as a loyal Christian all through the emergency in daily fear of his life. He was able to voice some of his own hopes, and the fears that he had lived through, in a very moving contribution. This was a great relief to him as to others present.

After the meeting the party was shown round the hospital wards. Mwariama seemed very surprised to see so many Africans being so well cared for, some of whom actually had been his own men in the forest. He was like a child, running from one bed to another in his delight. Three days later a forlorn little girl arrived at the hospital with a letter from Mwariama, written in English by a secretary. It asked us to admit his little daughter as a patient, but regretted he had no money to pay her fees. She was suffering from the effects of starvation and scabies, due to privations endured while 'on the run' with her family in the forest. We were indeed glad to help in further building up confidence and love. Only a week or so later we had the Field Marshal's own mother also as a patient in our wards, suffering from arthritis.

I felt that all this had been very much worthwhile. It is interesting that at the end of the meeting Mr Stanley had called for prayer, which he himself led. On my enquiring what the Fighters might think of that, I was told that 'All the Forest Fighters pray regularly' though they avoid using the name of Jesus, and say 'Yea' instead of 'Amen'.

Bewitched

I could find no organized temple or sign of pagan religion in Maua village. Perhaps I was blind, but of superstition and witchcraft there was plenty.

One day a woman was brought to me in O.P.D. She was gesturing and talking nonsense. Her family could not understand her. In the wards she was noisy, refused food and was filthy all the time. No drugs had any effect and she was a headache for everyone. Then after a couple of weeks a nurse on duty remarked to me that the woman had told her that she had been bewitched. Someone was trying to kill her. That was the cause of her trouble. Hearing this I got into touch with our elderly African minister, Rev. Jusufu. I asked him to come and pray with her. This he did on his next visit to Maua. He did it quite simply, briefly and unemotionally. I was standing alongside. Nothing special happened. From that moment she began very slowly, to improve. When the time came for my own departure she was quite well. A normal, quiet, helpful patient. But her family had left her with us to die. They were lost in their forest home, gone and no address. Hospital was trying to trace her home via the local chiefs. I have her photo taken when cured and waiting, just waiting for something to happen.

Staff Problems

Boy/girl relationships were very difficult in such a rapidly changing society as that of Kenya in 1964. During my four months at Maua we lost three promising girl students with pregnancies, and boys were dismissed. Another problem was to obtain enough qualified African staff. As soon as they graduate they move off to highly paid jobs in Government hospitals in the towns, with which a village mission hospital cannot compete.

In one case I felt that I had to intervene. A boy nurse was being severely, and I felt possibly unjustly, dealt with ... I shall never forget the fear and hate that I saw on his face as he passed me by. I followed him to his dormitory and sought him out. I said to him simply: 'I am your friend. You can come and talk to me at any time.' He took me at my word and came quietly next morning. We had a very useful chat. He has never forgotten that day when he found a friend. He still writes to me in England, though he is now in Government employ.

Maua gets a new Out-Patient Department

During my last weeks at Maua I spent my spare time drawing plans

188

for what I felt might be a much needed new building for out-patients. There was no prospect of any funds. A minimum cost of a conventional building would be £6,000. However, I contacted one of our agricultural workers who was producing concrete sectional buildings for his own work, and I revised my plans to fit his standard parts, thus more than halving probable costs. At that stage I left for home.

In Nairobi I stayed again with Mr Kendall. He had that day met a Government official of the hospitals department who reported having available for immediate use a sum of £700 if some hospital could meet it pound for pound. Could we accept this challenge, find the money and erect the first half of the planned standard building? We found that a gift of £300 had been promised and was due, and a few small balances, and between us we could foot the balance. Kendall, who is a trained engineer, then re-drew my amateur plans, took them next day to the Government Offices and got them accepted. The day I left on my plane, he went off to Maua and put the work in hand, as there was a deadline for using the money in the next two months. And so Maua had got the first half of its much needed O.P.D.; and the next year the scheme was completed. I wish I could see it!

Nigeria

Another short period of retirement in Staffordshire followed, and then in October, 1964, I found myself disembarking from a V.C.10 plane at Ibadan in Western Nigeria. Our son Andrew, was there to meet me.

Andrew had qualified in Medicine at Liverpool, and had worked for four years at Hankow, China, having to leave China only a week or so before ourselves. He was almost at once sent by our Mission to take charge of the Wesley Guild Hospital, Ilesha, Nigeria. Finding himself in 1964 very short of medical staff for that large hospital, he suggested that I might come out and perhaps work half-time for six months. The hospital could pay my fare and I would be at home with him. So that was it. The only snag was to find any 'half-days'. Every day was soon full of work, not to mention night calls.

Hospital work had been started by the missionaries at Ilesha in a very small way in 1913. About 1950, plans were made in co-operation with the local Yoruba Chiefs to remove the hospital to a large new site in virgin forest close to the town. In 1952 this scheme was just beginning to get under way and Andrew had to take it over. In the years since then he has seen it grow until it is now perhaps our busiest mission hospital anywhere. Its Out-Patient Department

189

handles over 1,000 cases every working morning. There are 130 In-Patient beds, with X-rays, Laboratory, operating theatre, maternity and child welfare schemes, etc., and branch dispensaries at Ikole, Imesi-Ile and Kaiama (200 miles away in Northern Nigeria). Also a large and fully equipped School of Nursing with 90 pupils.

My own work was in routine clinical tasks, some emergency operations, and in starting their first small Eye Clinic. I could also take my turn at the English language morning prayers in the hospital chapel, or at an occasional church service using an interpreter.

The Child Welfare work of this hospital is outstanding. A small Government subsidy for each case enables all patients under eighteen to be treated free. This has attracted such a response that it was recently found that over 95% of all the children in Ilesha town (population 150,000) now hold a hospital registration card. At Imesi-Ile every child in the village is sent by the Chief to the clinic regularly for the first five years. There a complete record of its development, feeding and illnesses is kept and the punch card records are to be analysed to try to find the causes of so much child mortality, Kwashiorkor, etc.

One of the big drug companies recently donated a large amount of the new measles vaccine (not yet in routine use in Great Britain), and the hospital is now attempting to make Ismesi-Ile the first village in the Tropics to be free of measles. In Africa measles is a much dreaded and often fatal disease when it occurs among the ill-nourished and devitaminized babies.

This Welfare work has recently had further recognition in that the big Government University at Ibadan is now sending all of its final-year medical students, two by two, for a week of study at Ilesha Hospital, where they get special instructions into the methods of Child Welfare Work and a look into hospital administration. The Save the Children Fund is also co-operating.

On one occasion while in Ilesha I sat in, as a full member, at the Ilesha Methodist 'Local Preachers' Meeting'. I was the only European amid a crowd of Africans, but they gave me a feeling welcome as being truly one of themselves. We duly passed two new Local Preachers from 'on trial' to 'full plan', just as in such a meeting at home. Perhaps I should add that all the church work is now in African hands. The few English ministers remaining are teachers or specialists of one kind or another.

It was a joy, so soon as I arrived in Ilesha, to find myself always addressed as 'Grandpa'. Andrew, their loved Superintendent, has long been known as 'Father', so of course, my superior title was, for an African, inevitable. Throughout the large mixed African and European staff there is such a free, happy atmosphere, that the whole hospital is like a big joyous family.

A Last Word

And so I come to a suitable place to end my story. At 76 I now rest in a backwater where life moves slowly. But I can still be useful in a few odd jobs.

Has it all been worth while? Yes, indeed, a thousand times worth while.

Living as Mary and I did, on the usual Methodist Living Allowance, small but regular, it sometimes seemed as though we were strangely isolated from the rough and tumble of the world around us. Can I ever understand, I wonder, the anxieties of a man out of work? Or whose business is going wrong despite his best efforts. Or the daily search for food which is the lot of so many Eastern peasants?

And there was always our home. Mary made that. Without her self-sacrificing co-operation I should have been a lame duck. All through the years of our marriage, whether we happened to be both in the same place, or separated by half the world for years together, she always faithfully did her part in the common task to which we were pledged. Her family today is her memorial, each in his or her different way living out her ideals.

We are now living in a new world. There are today new ways of service which did not exist in my young days. Jobs in commerce. Jobs in Government service in many of the new nations who need teachers, agricultural experts, engineers, etc., as well as many short service opportunities in the various Voluntary Service Organizations and the like, dozens of ways in which it is possible to give one's self. Whole-hearted love and service for others is *never* in vain. True, there are times when the proffered love seems to be thrown back in the giver's face. But what of that? Did not our Master suffer so?

To any who are trying to find the way of Jesus for themselves in the world today, I would say **'Get Up And Go'**, where and when the opportunity offers. Life is never going to be easy. It may be that you go in family harness, or it may be all alone. It may be far away, or it may be at home. It may be in youth, or perhaps in old age, but if God is calling you, throw in all you have and *go*. God will be there. He trusts *you*. He gives us each a job. Often it is in an unsympathetic or even a hostile world. Dare we fail Him?

191

Printed by Ernest J. Day & Co. Ltd., London and Bedford